WHEN ENERGY BECOMES FORM

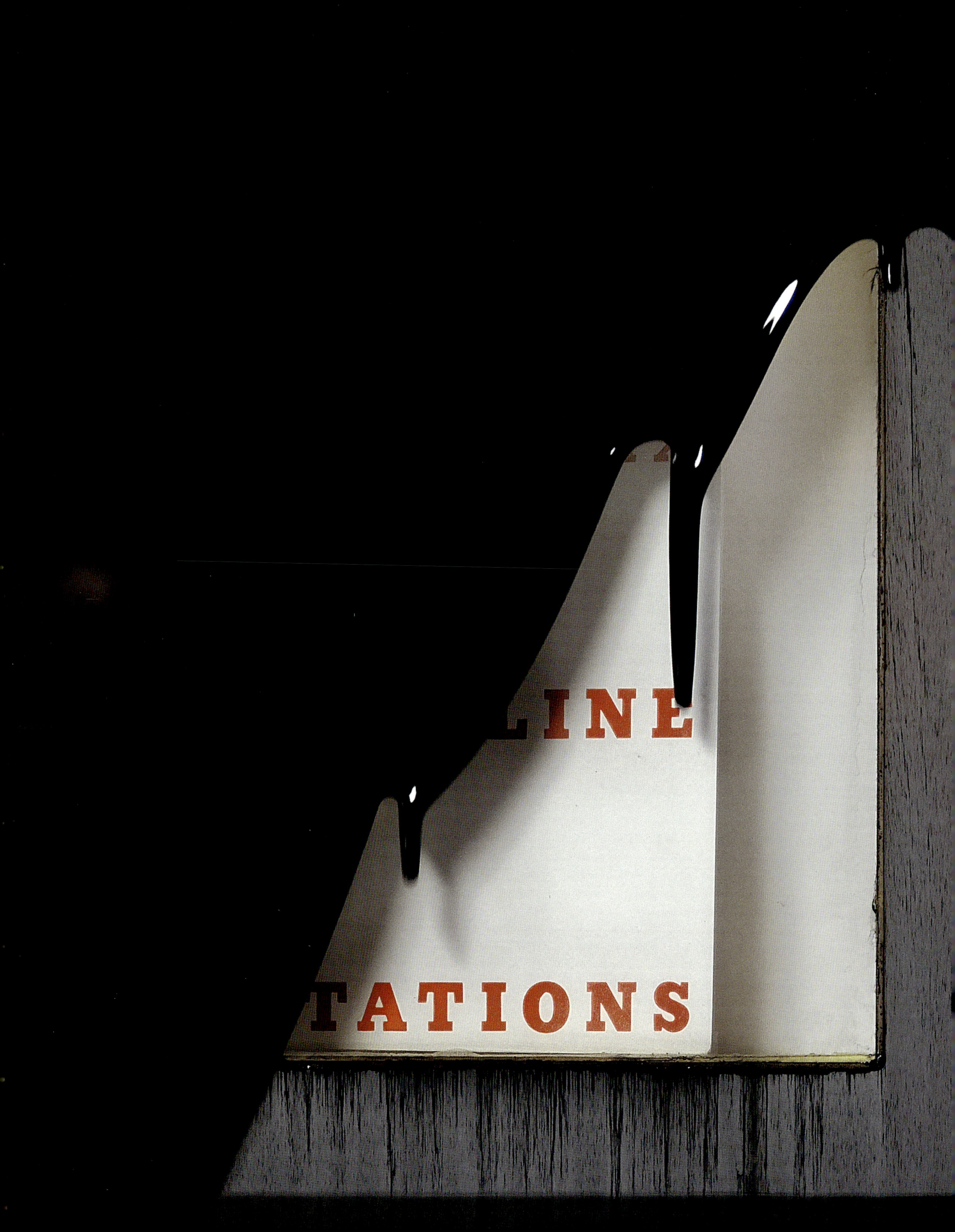

LINE
TATIONS

WHEN ENERGY BECOMES FORM

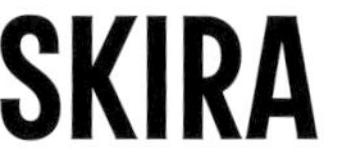

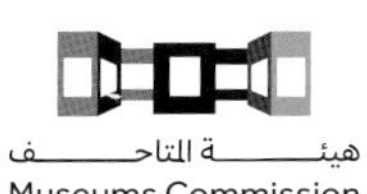

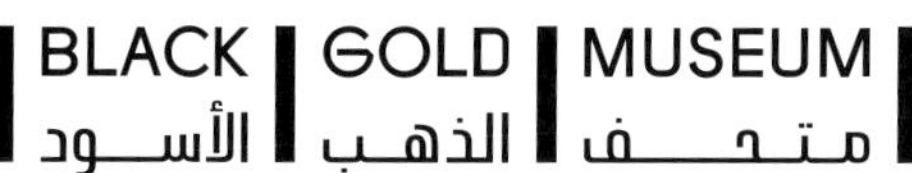

The inaugural exhibition *When Energy Becomes Form*
is presented at the Black Gold Museum
from 3 December 2025 to 28 February 2026.
Produced by the Museums Commission, Ministry of Culture,
Saudi Arabia.

**His Highness Prince Badr bin Abdullah bin Mohammed
bin Farhan Al Saud**
Minister of Culture

His Excellency Hamed bin Mohammed Fayez
Vice Minister of Culture

Mona Khazindar
Chief Advisor to the Minister of Culture

Artists
BP and Renaud Layrac

Curator
Christian Janicot

Scenography Design
Agence NC: Nathalie Crinière, Lucille Louveau,
Taoyu Wang

Design Management
Anne Jaffrennou
Stéphane Berthier

Lighting Design
Lightemotion: François Roupignan, Maricar Bustamante

Audiovisual Design
La Méduse
Richard Cailleux
Nokinomo

Museum Graphic and Signage
Anamorphée: Charlotte Halpern, Inès Osni

Production
Direct Line

BLACK GOLD MUSEUM

Jack Persekian
Director

Souha Aldowalibi
Project Coordination

Ahmed Alharbi
Administrative Affairs and Operations Support, Manager

Zena Alshehri
Education and Community Engagement, Manager

Dana Kushari
Administrative Affairs and Operations Support, Specialist

Nasser Alqahtani
Logistics Support, Specialist

MUSEUMS COMMISSION

Ibrahim Alsanousi
Acting CEO, Museums Commission

Sylvain Fort
General Manager of Museums and Assets Department

Jane Smythe
Head of Research and Publications Department

Hagar Adam
Research and Publications Department, Senior Specialist

Virginia Cassola
Director of Curatorial Collections

Iman Ibrahim
Digital Documentation, Team Lead

Jana Jabbour
Director of Communication and Media

Attia Alrajhi
Public Relations, Manager

Nuwayyir Alotaibi
Communication Department, Content Developer

Budoor Alrubayan
Communication Department, Design Manager

Hussein Al Abbad
Director of Museum and Assets Operations

Abdullah Alfaifi
Logistics and Operations, Manager

List of lenders
Frac Alsace, Sélestat
Centre Pompidou (MNAM), Paris
Christian Berthier
Galerie Louis Carré
Géotec Dijon
MAMAC, Nice
Marc Faggionato
Renaud Layrac

MONA KHAZINDAR

Chief Advisor to the Minister of Culture

PREFACE

It is with great pride that the Museums Commission inaugurates the Black Gold Museum with an exhibition that is as daring as it is timely – *When Energy Becomes Form*. This exhibition invites us to reflect on the past that has shaped our identity and to envision the future we aspire to build, both culturally and materially. It is a privilege to welcome the French artist collective BP, whose body of work reimagines petroleum not merely as a resource, but as a symbol, a material, and a subject of artistic reflection.

Saudi Arabia's history is closely intertwined with oil, which catalyzed our transformation into a modern nation and positioned us at the crossroads of energy, culture, and global influence. As we now forge a new narrative through Vision 2030 -- one rooted in innovation, creativity, and cultural enrichment – it is fitting that this exhibition invites us to reflect critically on the very material that shaped our recent past.

Spanning over four decades, the BP Art Collection is full of different meanings and perspectives, all while keeping a touch of wit and playfulness. Their installations, sculptures, and images challenge us to reconsider oil not just as an industrial product, but as a cultural force – dense with meaning, memory, and contradiction. Through their ironic lens, barrels become architecture, fuel pumps become metaphors, and used oil becomes an expressive medium of decay and transformation.

As we open the doors of the Black Gold Museum, we do more than unveil an exhibition – we ignite a conversation. One that acknowledges the complexity of our past while embracing the creative potential of our future. May this moment mark the beginning of many encounters that push boundaries, challenge perceptions, and inspire generations to come.

CHRISTIAN JANICOT

Curator

WHEN ENERGY BECOMES FORM

For the inaugural exhibition of the Black Gold Museum, *When Energy Becomes Form*, the goal was to invite the French artist collective BP. Presenting this group, whose unique work is based on the appropriation and diversion of petroleum, felt like a natural choice. Who better than these creators to showcase petroleum and reveal its true nature? What more fitting setting than a retrospective in Saudi Arabia, the heart of the kingdom of black gold?

Founded in the early 1980s, BP emerged unexpectedly when Renaud Layrac, Frédéric Pohl, and Richard Bellon discovered stickers from the oil company British Petroleum and decided to adopt them as their signature.

From then on, their production focused exclusively on the world of oil: repurposing materials from the oil and automotive industries, creating installations with industrial objects – barrels, cans, gas pumps – and experimenting with used oil as a medium.

In 1984, their first work, *Trois monochromes,* enclosed used oil at various stages of aging in glass panels. Two years later, *Peinture* à *l'huile* (1986) featured a pump dripping a viscous liquid onto a metal panel. Their monumental installations multiplied: a mock oil rig was built near a service station; another was installed on the hills of Nice, topped with a neon flame. In 1986, *Stock* amassed 150 barrels in a Hamburg parking lot, initiating a play of scale and structure. From then on, their works transformed the barrel into a sculptural element, isolated or stacked, as in *Babel* (1987), evoking ancient architecture, or in *Untitled* (1987), where used oil slowly flows and oozes from the barrel.

There's a playful energy to BP's work, a lighthearted approach that subtly mocks the end of the avant-garde, the end of the Trente Glorieuses, and modernist utopias. A famous Parisian gallery owner even nicknamed them *Les garagistes,* highlighting the collective's ironic sensibility.

BP was exceptionally ahead of its time.

Forty years on, BP remains a distillation of art and energy! BP continues to intrigue with its strict, self-imposed constraints within the art world. With its work *Black/Gold* (2006), a golden brass plaque with a square of dripping oil at its center, BP becomes a mirror of our contemporary reflections.

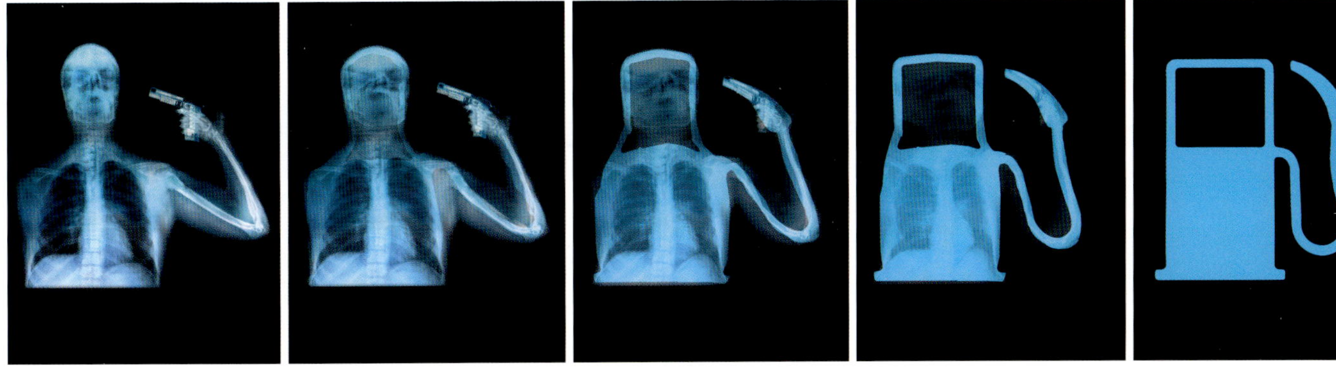

Ahmed Mater. *Evolution of Man,* 2011. Digital print, Custom Made Lightbox, 83 × 62 × 7 cm each. Courtesy of the artist

This exhibition showcases the resonance between BP's work and that of Saudi artist Ahmed Mater, specifically comparing their respective pieces, *Serpent* and *Evolution of Man*, where the fuel pump hose is diverted from its primary function, evoking both amusement and contemplation.

In selecting works for this inaugural exhibition, the term "immersion" immediately came to mind – a concept too hastily associated with digital experiences today, as if art history had never produced immersive installations before the digital age. Here, the immersion is not virtual, but material: a sensory dive into the fluid's density, its brown reflections, and its magnificent, tactile, and moving materiality.

To my knowledge, BP remains the only collective to have truly "assimilated" oil, to the point of artistically refining it and making it the very essence of their artistic language. More than a mere material, the artists transformed it into a symbolic substance, a marker of civilization, an element of both fascination and critique, with its ambivalence revealed in each work – between power and dependence, opacity and light, industry and art.

Oil is the source of the BP art group; oil is the resource of Saudi Arabia. But this is not merely a semantic parallel; it points to a fundamental truth: oil fuels existence, it is the engine driving both artistic expression and economic systems.

Saudi Arabia's central role in the history of petroleum is well recognized. The discovery of oil in the 1930s marked a turning point, rooting the Kingdom firmly within the course of the modern world's progress. This resource, far more than an economic engine, has enabled the development of infrastructure, institutions, and cultural exchanges on an unprecedented scale. Today, the Kingdom is embarking on a new era, investing in innovation, energy diversification, and the dialogue between tradition and the future.

This perspective offers a particularly interesting prism through which to view the work of BP. This dialogue between past and future is part of the new identity that Renaud Layrac has given to BP, the only member to continue the collective's legacy since 2008. The acronym now stands for *Before Present*, in reference to Carbon-14 dating.

His *Horizons d'attente* (2019), a series of photographs in which industrial landscapes – from thermal power stations and oil fields to wind farms and solar installations – outline the various potential trajectories of the energy world, oscillating between fossil heritage and future alternatives. His *Petrographies* explore the question of time through a process of image recycling. He takes shots of oil installations, refineries, highways, and interchanges, taken from industrial archives or simply gleaned from the Internet.

For this exhibition at the Black Gold Museum, Renaud Layrac, continuing the BP legacy, has produced three new *Petrographies*. For *Petrography (archive 1)* and *Petrography (archive 2),* they appropriate images of Aramco's aesthetically pleasing oil installations from the 1950s, located in the Eastern Province of Saudi Arabia. By engraving deep black traces into the photographic material, like a series of pipelines zigzagging without beginning or end, the artist questions oil's place within the landscape, the kingdom's history, and the broader history of art.

In *Pétrographie (raffinerie 1)*, the Jubail refinery complex serves as inspiration, with the artist inscribing traces of a changing world, a green, assertive road between memory and reinvention. As Saudi Arabia reimagines its energy future with initiatives such as Vision 2030, we can clearly recognize the echo of the energy created by a new path.

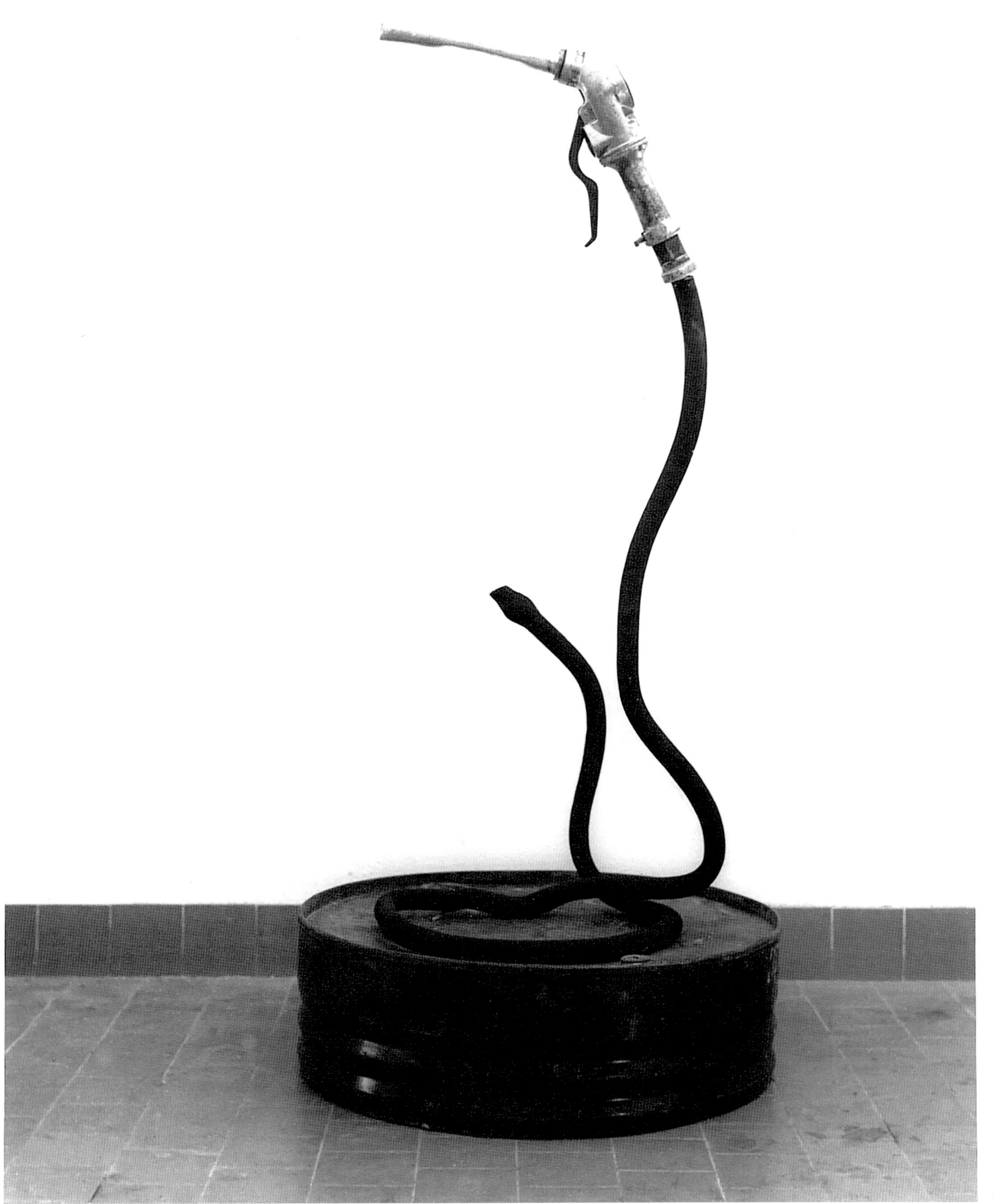

ARNAULD PIERRE

THE CULT OF MODERN DEITIES

In the early 1980s, Renaud Layrac, Frédéric Pohl, and Richard Bellon were students at Villa Arson in Nice, a school and art center known for its vibrancy. When they started working together, they viewed their association as like being in a rock band – in which, incidentally, they also played. The three friends painted and collectively signed large canvases of figurative and abstract motifs mixed with strong material effects. Nothing has survived of this youthful output, created not just at the school's workshops but in a garage that the father of Bellon's girlfriend lent them. In this garage, the trio came across some old stickers from the British Petroleum oil company. Commonly displayed by motorists on the rear of their vehicles, stuck on the windshield, or directly on the bodywork, these advertising images were pared back to the famous green and yellow shield-shaped logo, designed by Raymond Loewy in the 1950s in an Adrien Frutiger typeface: the company's initials, BP. The three friends decided there and then to use this striking logotype as their signature, affixing these stickers to the bottom of their own canvases... and that was how the BP group came into being.[2]

"I love the stuff, oil"
Michel Magne and Jean Yanne, "Petrol Pop," 1973[1]

With corporate ideology in the ascendancy in an increasingly neo-liberal world, the BPs began working at a time when, repudiating the tyranny of the individual signature, artists deliberately concealed their identities behind false corporate names. One pioneer was the General Idea group from Canada, operating at the very end of the 1960s with an artmaking approach based on a vocabulary of consumer society, advertising, and mass media signs. Back in France, the IFP (Information Fiction Publicité) trio, active between 1983 and 1994, readily comes to mind; group member Philippe Thomas (in complete anonymity) in 1987 went on to set up the fictitious "Readymades Belong to Everyone®" agency in New York. Philippe Cazal, on the other hand, first commissioned a real communication agency to logotypize his own name, then concealed his name behind the registered trademark "L'artiste dans son milieu®." Appropriating the BP name and logo was emblematic of another 1980s art trend: a critical stance toward the inevitable commodification of contemporary art, at a time of exploding art market speculation. Before the decade was out, Ashley Bickerton's minimalist objects, reminiscent of artwork transportation crates, were covered over with stickers and logos as if to flaunt their perfect adaptation to the increasing circulation of artworks in the economic sphere. Opposing the myth of inspirational creation to the mercantilism of mass production, Bickerton came up with a manufacturer's name, "Susie," which he used in lieu of his signature, soon making it a registered trademark.

The Nice-based trio's approach differed from that of their contemporaries in the astonishing intentionality of the name they had chosen. BP is not just a signature, it is the name of a project; in vanishingly few artistic enterprises does the signature precede the work to such an extent, in the process guaranteeing utter coherence. Once chosen, the BP group's signature determined a clear direction, sharply circumscribing the specific field of formal and thematic investigation. With that name, everything fell into place: the trio acted in accordance with the brand, delving exclusively into the world of oil exploitation, products, techniques and infrastructure, and of course the detail that made it all possible – evolution of a car-based society. BP's members eschewed painting for ready-mades, employing metal drums and oil cans from various brands, kerosene lamps, gas pumps, car hoods, and tires, motorcycle helmets, cones, traffic signs, safety barriers... Rather than using the traditional painters' medium, they used waste oils or hydraulic fluids, effectively creating a new form of "oil painting." The BPs first showed their work before graduation, at a group exhibition on the theme of time: a triptych of monochromes, each panel featuring used oil at various stages of ageing, from clearer to darker (*Trois monochromes*, 1984). In 1919, Dadaist Francis Picabia painted *M'amenez-y*, a large mechanomorphic canvas covered in inscriptions, bad puns ridiculing the artist's profession and a certain idea of painting; the most visible inscription at the top of the work announced: "castor oil painting!" alluding to a particularly unpalatable medicinal concoction. In 1986, the year when the trio graduated, the BPs "waste oil painting" found a new and equally ironic iteration in the form of a metallic painting apparently completely sprayed with a viscous, blackish liquid (*Peinture à l'huile*, 1986) by an exposed electric pump. Prior to this, the group took part in a collective exhibition at an associative space near a gas station. At the entrance, they built a fake wooden derrick topped with a sign announcing the event. They repeated the exercise soon afterward, at Fort du Mont Alban, overlooking the city of Nice, erecting a derrick six or seven meters tall, this time crowned with a flame of neon tubes.

The first time BP used metal drums was also in 1986, when they installed a hundred and fifty of them in a parking lot in Hamburg, Germany, under the evocative title, *Stock*. Accumulation-based approaches were still exceptional at the time. More often than not, they presented ready-made drums in isolation, as in *Untitled* (1987) at the musée national d'Art moderne at the Centre Pompidou, dripping with waste oil collected in a hollow base; or scaffolded with a few counterparts into columns of varying heights, allowing the drum to express its constructive and architectural connotations (the "shaft" of a column). As the title indicates, *Babel* (1987) stacked four barrels of decreasing size and diameter, giving the work a ziggurat-style silhouette potentially evocative of Middle Eastern architectural structures from ancient times, long before the discovery of oil. In *Noir et Blanc* (1987), the four stacked barrels' alternating sizes, colors and textures interrupt the vertical momentum of another *Colonne* (1987) over three meters high, with six stacked barrels, the first of which – wider and taller – forming the base. Occasionally, they arranged regular stacks of plastic oil cans solo rather than in columns, forming rectangular-sectioned pillars of an equally architectural appearance (*Mobil*, 1988). These isolated columns also convey connotations beyond the constructive: in isolation, they assume the form and function of votive or commemorative columns, erected in memory of an event or a person, or in service of some cult or another. The approach further developed in a work installed in 1988 at the Tourcoing Art School, one that (in every sense of the term) dominates this first series of vertical structures: a square-sectioned metallic stack dripping with waste oil, topped by a single, intact drum adorned with the BP wings, nearly four meters above the ground. So elevated, the barrel looms over us, metonymically embodied in the object tasked with containing it and in the substance that appears to drip from it onto its supporting base. In an untitled work the following year, rather than being elevated, the barrel sits in the middle of a small tank barely big enough to contain it, now stripped, trickling with new oil whose golden color bestows the same degree of sacredness.

Not that the worship of modern gods, to which the trio ironically devoted themselves, was anything new. Written at a time when automobile traffic was growing and becoming democratically accessible, Surrealist Louis Aragon noted in *Le Paysan de Paris* how roadside oratories and calvaries where travelers had once stopped were disappearing, replaced by "great red gods, great yellow gods, great green gods," gas pumps before which followers of speed were now compelled to stop:

> These idols have a kinship that makes
> them formidable. Emblazoned in
> English with newly-created words,
> equipped with one long, flexible arm,
> a luminous faceless head, a single foot
> and a belly with a numbered wheel, gas

pumps sometimes borrow the appearance of an Ancient Egyptian deity, of some anthropophagous tribe that worships only war.[3]

He immediately launched into this invocation: "O Texaco Motor Oil, Eco, Shell, great inscriptions of human potential! Soon shall we cross ourselves before your fountains…"[4] The evocative power of Aragon's images, their use of shapes, color and the heraldry of oil companies – very early on, and not just BP! – brings to mind certain images from the Pop era, such as Allan D'Arcangelo's roads flanked by the logos of major oil companies; in the quadriptych *Full Moon* (1962), an exaggerated perspective draws the viewer's gaze toward the progressive rise of a celestial body which, in actual fact, is the circular Gulf Oil Company emblem. Notably, in Ed Ruscha's painting *Standard Station, Amarillo, Texas* (1963), an exaggerated perspective brings the service station's solemn gas pumps into the foreground. In the same period, Ruscha collected twenty-six gas station views from California to Oklahoma, along a route he travelled often, explicitly likening them to secular stations of the cross, for publication in his first photo book.[5] Having adapted a number of images from this book in a series of graphite and motor oil drawings (*Untitled*, 2000), the BP group artists were quite familiar with this work. A 2008 piece features a reprint, set behind the glass of a painting periodically obscured by an electric pump streaming a completely opaque curtain across it, in a gesture that straddles homage, desecration, irony, and ambiguity.

These are the "fountains" before which Aragon promised motorists would cross themselves; fountains no longer generated by pure water from sacred sources, replaced by black blood from the bowels of the earth, source of merely temporal wealth. Technically speaking, many of the BP group's works are fountains, iterations of endless closed motor oil circuits. The series began with *Oil line*, a guardrail along a nearly twenty-meter-long slope, installed in 1986 at Villa Arson; the liquid flowed through a central groove, perpetually pumped by an electric pump back up to the starting point. By the same process, the viscous, shiny substance is constantly overflowing from barrels that have been transformed into cornucopias of a new kind. The one that BP had installed in 1988 in Aarau in the middle of a circular pond ten meters in diameter gave the impression of a self-generated profusion. Another work from 1988 was left open to give viewers a glimpse of the oil's internal flow, creating an apparently bottomless well,

a Danaides' barrel from which the precious substance may indefinitely be drawn. A contemporary fountain ejecting fluid from new sacred sources, gas pumps put in an appearance in replicas made in 1987 and 1988: one pump contemplates its reflection in a pool of oil at its base; the other offers the viewer a mirror, its front replaced with a dark, reflective spill. The "long and flexible arm" completing the body of these modern deities as Aragon depicted them was repurposed in an early BP work, in which a pump nozzle and hose are poised like a serpent over a small drum (*Serpent*, 1986).

Reflecting on belief systems and practices known as religions, French sociologist Émile Durkheim wrote that sacred things must be set apart from the secular world.[6] Indeed, it is by this that we recognize them: the fact that the staging generates extreme attraction, while maintaining a distance, in a dialectic of the near and the far that, according to another thinker, Walter Benjamin, is the source of the aura that surrounds them.[7] As we have had occasion to note, plinths and bases ensured the visibility of fetishes BP offered up to parodic adoration, in part keeping them in a space that is not ours, not of mere mortals. The framing fulfils this function in other works too. After that first exposed mechanism *Peinture à l'huile*, BP presented oily monochromes in frames that, concealing all equipment, reinforced the mystery of how their strange surfaces were generated, helping to focus the gaze while preserving their own space – especially when the frame takes on large-scale proportions, as in the untitled work (1990) for the Fond national d'art contemporain, and in works where the framing is provided by life-size car hoods. In other pieces, the frame is made up of traffic signs in which red arrows are deliberately directed at the monochrome, an effective way of alerting the observer to the significant value of what they are being invited to look at. Other works highlight their constituent parts, objects placed on shelves like small altars, conducive to private acts of devotion. Thus, we encounter a warning triangle, a tire or a beacon light, in untitled works from 1990 and 1992, displayed alongside the icon par excellence in BP's work since the start: a black square dripping with oil.

The most effective auratic devices BP invented, engendering the highest degree of fascination and repulsion, are the ones that use waste oil as their main medium. An amalgam of all seductions, the waste oil is soft and silky to the eye, its depth and reflections in balance, as in a Pierre Soulages' *Outrenoir*, and yet it stays at a distance, untouchable; to approach it is to risk contamination, an indelible stain. Durkheim states:

"The sacred thing is, par excellence, that which the profane must not and cannot touch with impunity."[8] The etymology reminds us: for the Romans, the word *sacer* meant both "consecrated to the gods" and "laden with filth"; thus, the noble and the ignoble are indistinctly mixed in the sacred. Due to its untouchable nature, the seductive and repugnant substance establishes a prohibition, reinforcing the aura of sacredness around some of the works, insofar as "sacred things are those protected and isolated by prohibitions."[9] It is in this respect – and not merely for vague formal reasons, such as the predominance of verticality – that their works may be seen as totems, imbued with the tutelary power constitutive of any totem, which is essentially taboo, consubstantially attached to a prohibition. The totemic power here, of course, belongs to oil. All the objects and substances BP mobilized are underpinned by oil, as if members of the same clan, which are straightforwardly different modalities of the totemic Being, albeit not sharing with it the same character of sacredness.[10] More recently, a series of photographs taken in the business districts of Paris-La Défense, Frankfurt, and London has borne out modern civilization's penchant for totemic output, a slew of skyscrapers emblazoned with the name of their tutelary entity: EDF, Total, GDF Suez, Ernst & Young, and Deutsche Bahn (*Sky Zero,* 2011).

Aragon long ago warned us that the sacred in question here manifests in a form that is considerably devalued and secularized, mere simulacra, hence his reference to the "great gods" with which we might confuse roadside gas pumps: "Strange statuary presides over the birth of these simulacra,"[11] he writes, the primary meaning of simulacrum being "image or idols." The simulacrum was a pre-eminent artworld concern in the 1980s, a decade that opened with French philosopher Jean Baudrillard's work, *Simulacres et Simulation* (1981), extending the Marxist critique of commodity fetishism, that is, "fetishism attached to the products of labor presented as commodities."[12] Simulationism denominated a whole segment of art at this time, presenting simple consumer objects as veritable commodity fetishes, for example, Jeff Koons' Hoover-branded vacuum cleaners encased in impeccable minimalist Plexiglas boxes, bathed in a sanctifying halo of light emitted by fluorescent tubes (*New Hoover Convertible,* 1980). By 1979, fetishized merchandise was invading the New York arts scene as it became the center of the art market, notably Haim Steinbach's first *Displays* lining up brand-new household objects and kitschy decorative items in serial arrangements on Formica shelves, offered up for adoration like modern gods on the altars of a secular religion, a presentation mode already employed by the BP group who were, evidently enough, not unaware of American Simulationist art. This certainly applied to their orderly presentations, aestheticizing the ready-made and obeying certain rules of minimal art, such as repetition and modularity. Two untitled 1991 works housed alternating white and black motorcycle helmets in metal shelving compartments, with orthogonal uprights creating a grid. The resulting three-dimensional version of a black-and-white checkerboard was directly inspired by racing flags, which also feature in other works from that period. The group deployed the same repetitive arrangement in at least two works in which oil lamps are aligned: one (*Untitled,* 1988) was a diptych, juxtaposing a 3 x 3 lamp panel with an oil painting made using waste oil; an untitled work from 1990 arranged three Yacco-branded oil cans at regular intervals under three small paintings, serially juxtaposing objects related to paintings, citing the classic vocabulary of abstraction, as adopted by European Simulationist John M. Armleder, who around that time was producing a combination of ready-mades and painting – a combination that had much to say about the place pictorial references occupied in fetishization processes at work everywhere in art during this period.

The BP group has systematically associated the equally demystified worship of the fetishes of modern art with the worship of commercial gods and their all-encompassing tutelary power in the form of oil. Framing three monochromes in waste oil with colors reminiscent of Neoplasticism, as in *Red, Yellow and Blue* from 1993, the BP group effectively drew Piet Mondrian into the purity- and impurity-based dialectic long central to their work. A nod to Mondrian was also evident in a 1995 piece in which, each in a primary color, three motorcycle helmets appear to contemplate the monochrome the artists placed before them. The title of this piece, *Sportsmen,* not only referenced this work but also harked back to Kazimir S. Malevich's 1930–31 painting of the same name, which depicts four figures in silhouette, segmented into planes of pure color, their heads reduced to geometric form. The BP group's arrangement of the helmets sought out this visual echo. Malevich consistently served as a touchstone in the BP group's oeuvre, including several *Black Squares* rendered in waste oil, playfully subverting the iconic Modernist work: *Black Square on White Background*, which the Suprematist master displayed at the seminal 1915 *0.10* exhibition in Saint Petersburg. Reiterating this unmistakable reference, the BP group revisited Suprematism's core shapes – the square, the cross, and the circle – in 1990 in three graphite and waste oil drawings, stained by spreading halos of oil on paper. In some initial diversions, BP placed the sticky square within grids of black and white, evoking the pattern of a car racing flag and generic forms of geometric abstraction, with a particular nod to Mondrian in their untitled 1991 work, which features a square frame tilted on its corner. A later work, from 2005, features a square that precisely mirrors the angle of Malevich's *White Square on White Background* (1918), continuing the Malevich reference in a way that blurs the line between tribute and satire.

These initial forays into the Modernist tradition were soon complemented by references to postwar abstraction. By the late 1990s, several BP artworks were configured as mechanical dripping pieces, in which the act of painting mimicked Jackson Pollock's technique, reduced to a parody reminiscent of a malfunctioning engine with a machine spraying oil behind a glass pane. The automated mechanical process usurped the physical and psychological automatism celebrated by Pollock, stripping away the sanctity of the gestural act foundational to Abstract Expressionism and a whole cult of art that revered originality and authenticity through spontaneity. Moreover, all of the BP group's waste oil paintings function like painting machines that cease to flow, revealing their substrate once the electric pump feeding them is switched off. This concept was already evident in *Fontana* (1989), in which a metal frame pitted with holes alluded to the Italian master's punctured monochromes in his oeuvre *Buchi*. The name "Fontana" (Italian for "fountain") cleverly refers to the operational mode of these waste oil paintings which, as we've seen, resemble fountains. Adept at employing ready-mades, it was a natural progression for BP to follow in the footsteps of Marcel Duchamp, who famously transformed a white porcelain urinal into his celebrated artwork, *Fountain*, in 1917. The BP group's monochrome *LHMBP* (the acronym stands for Liquid Hydraulic Mineral British Petroleum, 1989) stacked two double-glazed plates filled with the titular greenish fluid, constructing a piece that inevitably recalls Duchamp's *Large Glass*.

An untitled 1989 work inverted a Solex moped's front wheel, embedding it in a barrel dripping with oil, in an even more overt nod to Duchamp's initiation of the ready-made series with *Bicycle Wheel* (1913); it also recalled how sculptor Jean Tinguely extended this gesture in the early 1960s through a number of mechanical assemblages. Tinguely brings to mind the New Realists – several of whom hailed from the south of France, either Nice or Marseille – where BPs began their career. Arman and César, in particular, had already worked with materials from the automotive industry, erecting totems just as deliberately critical of the personal automobile, consumer society's most consummate fetish. A 1992 BP installation in Nice accumulated car body panels in all colors behind a fence, presenting them frontally, à la Arman. Bulgarian-born artist Christo used oil barrels back in the late 1950s for his first wrappings; he went on to block Rue Visconti in Paris with barrels in 1961, as part of a solo exhibition at the Iris Clert Gallery. In the early 1960s, another artist from the south of France, Bernar Venet, presented effective examples of monochromes desublimated by a covering of vile, repulsive material: thick layers of tar that rendered the canvas a malodorous, evolving object, much like BP's waste oil monochromes later on.

The worship of modern fetishes is, as we have seen, a desublimating cult that may easily veer into iconoclasm. This is evident in the crumpled sheet metal surrounding some of the BP group's 1993 black squares, which have seemingly endured assaults of destructive violence against the icon they were assigned to protect – in some cases, in vain: one untitled monochrome from that year is nothing more than a pitifully crushed and crumpled rag. This may make us think of César's *Compressions*, and BP group contemporary, New Yorker Steven Parrino, who created pleated, crumpled, tortured monochromes with similar iconoclastic intent, directed against the idealism established by the monochrome genre during a spell of its history – between Malevich's position, a kind of spiritualism conceived to renew the powers of painting, and Aleksander M. Rodchenko's temptation to put it to death. In *Crash* (1994), a column of three steel parallelepipeds coated in red, yellow, and blue lacquer fully coincides with neoplasticism, the dented form giving the impression of a collision with a speeding vehicle. The title is evocative of James G. Ballard's 1973 novel and director David Cronenberg's film adaptation nearly a quarter-century later, which deals with the erotic encounter of bodies and automotive technology. This theme was once again the subject of photographs in the *Good Year* calendar (1991, the title alluding to the famous tire brand), for which BP staged female models at a car scrapyard. *Crash* more broadly established the theme of accidentology the BP group had begun exploring in their work at the start of the decade, including works behind a pane of glass sprayed regularly with oil and the spectral heads of crash test dummies, modern vanities that force us to remember the deadly flipside of the automotive dream.

Memento mori, remember that you will die, the dark silhouettes of the *Anonymes* series (1996) tell us, outlined in the manner of corpses laid out along the roadside by the great massacre of traffic accidents, which at that time in France had reached alarming proportions. An untitled 1992 work explored a similar theme: a simple still life composed of burnt-out automotive wreckage, exuding an undeniable sense of dread. The same sense of foreboding assailed viewers of an untitled 1994 work in which the ghost of a motorcyclist, represented by an empty suit suspended within a glass case, intermittently appears and vanishes with each spray of engine oil.

BP emerged in the period just after the optimistic "Trente Glorieuses" boom years, when the oil-fueled global economy seemed to be speeding along a limitless path.[13] The oil crises of the 1970s left their mark; the first Gulf War broke out in 1990; environmental catastrophes began to appear more frequently. The path to progress turned into a road to perdition, a *Highway To Hell* (1991) that wasn't just a hit song by Australian rock band AC/DC, it was also the title of a BP installation at the 1992 Sydney Biennale,[14] where five metal drums form the bases of an array of missiles pointing upright, a somber twist on Constantin Brancusi's serene and harmless *Birds in Space*. With conflict reignited in the Gulf a decade later, BP produced a series of reliefs with waste oil dripping in vertical streaks from metal letters that spell out the words "freedom," "democracy," "job is done" – weeping letters that lament the emptiness of slogans, reducing the grandest of intentions to no more than barcode-like insignia. In 2002, in a project titled *Produits dérivés*, the group launched two T-shirts featuring the names "Erika" and "Prestige" in a chic, fashion-magazine aesthetic and typeface. The stylishness barely conceals a reference to devastating oil spills caused by two tankers bearing these names, which foundered respectively off the coasts of Brittany in 1999 and Galicia in 2002. A subsequent installation, *Forêt Noire*, presented a collection of large wooden silhouettes shaped like tree-shaped air fresheners usually dangled from a car mirror. These ones were, however, saturated with waste oil and bitumen, serving as a stark reminder of acid rain pollution in Germany's Black Forest. BP group works and designs from the 2000s and beyond are, in essence, polluted works, a blend of graphite and oil that permeates to the quick of the paper fibers, akin to an oil slick, blurring the motifs the artists repurpose: corporate logos, including BP's own, turned into an ironic flower under the slogan "flower power," as well as traffic signage and, in a twist of irony, ecological icons like the World Wildlife Fund and the recycling symbol. In works like *Planisphere* (2007) and *Map (projection polaire)*, (2017), the coastlines of every continent are overrun by a spreading tide of engine oil; everything is tainted, nothing remains sacred.

Today, as we face the certainty of "the hour of the last barrel,"[15] BP's work takes on an ever-deepening significance. Emerging in the context of Simulationism and postmodern irony, with relentless consistency and clarity BP's works have dissected the simulacra upon which the world we know is built – a world vanishing before our eyes. Without slogans, without others' unequivocal messages, through the sheer power of form and staging, BP enable viewers to grasp meanings imbued with the weight and direction of history. With hindsight, their works eschew the carefree ambiance of the 1980s, revealing themselves to be highly critical, final expressions of the myths of a modernity that is necessarily and inevitably, receding. The most recent BP works – since 2008, carried forward by Renaud Layrac solo, recycle images onto which the artist superimposes obliterating signs. *Pétrographies*, as he calls them, are views of oil installations, refineries, and extraction fields, as well as highway networks and interchanges, sourced from oil company archives or the Internet. A succession of details betrays their age: not just the car models or oil workers' clothing styles, but the black-and-white, grainy images, certain types of framing, and compositional stylings of a bygone era: dated images of a past that once seemed full of promise, pinpointing the reality of a future whose terms are continually being redefined. The issue of time – time passed, a time announced that will never come to pass, time yet to come – lies at the heart of a new brand, one that Layrac conceived and launched under the unchanged acronym of BP, which now stands for "Before Present," a reference to Carbon-14 dating. The new logo appears on the *Horizons d'attente* series (2019), photographs of landscapes occupied by industrial facilities dedicated to energy production or transport, some still tied to fossil fuels (thermal power plants or extraction wells), others (nuclear power plants, wind turbines, or solar panels) pointing to potential alternatives. Will the horizon continue to darken, or, on the contrary, will it brighten? Well, for that we may only look to our "horizon of expectation."

1   "J'aime ça, le pétrole," Michel Magne and Jean Yanne's song "Petrol Pop" featured on the original soundtrack of Jean Yanne's film *Moi y'en a vouloir des sous*, a biting satire on labor union unrest in post-1968 France, on theatrical release in France in 1973.

2   The BP group continued as a trio until 1991, when Richard Bellon stepped back, followed by Frédéric Pohl in 2008. Final founding member Renaud Layrac is today custodian of the BP flame.

3   Louis Aragon, *Le Paysan de Paris* [1926], (Paris: Gallimard, 2018), 144–145.

4   *Ibid.*

5   Louise Katzman and Robert Whyte, *I Don't Want No Retro Spective: The Works of Edward Ruscha*, exh. cat., (San Francisco: Museum of Art-Hudson Hills Press, 1982), 19.

6   Émile Durkheim, *Les formes élémentaires de la vie religieuse* [1912], (Paris: Presses Universitaires de France, 1960), 50–51.

7   Walter Benjamin, "The Work of Art in the Age of Mechanical Reproducibility (1939, final version)," *Works III*, translated from German by Maurice de Gandillac, Rainer Rochlitz, and Pierre Rusch, (Paris: Gallimard, 2000), 280.

8   Émile Durkheim, *Les formes élémentaires*, op. cit., 55.

9   *Ibid.*, 56.

10   *Ibid.*, 213.

11   Louis Aragon, *Le Paysan de Paris*, op. cit., 145.

12   Karl Marx, *Le Capital. Livre 1* [1867], (Paris: Flammarion, 1999), 69.

13   Jean Fourastié coined this term for the period of growth France and the Western world experienced, from post-WWII to the mid-1970s, in *Les Trente Glorieuses* [1979], (Paris: Fayard, 2011).

14   Where, alongside Philippe Thomas and ORLAN, BP represented France.

15   Tagada Jones is a French punk metal band founded in Rennes in 1993; their track "Le dernier baril" is on the *À feu et à sang* album (Enrage Production, 2020).

WORKS

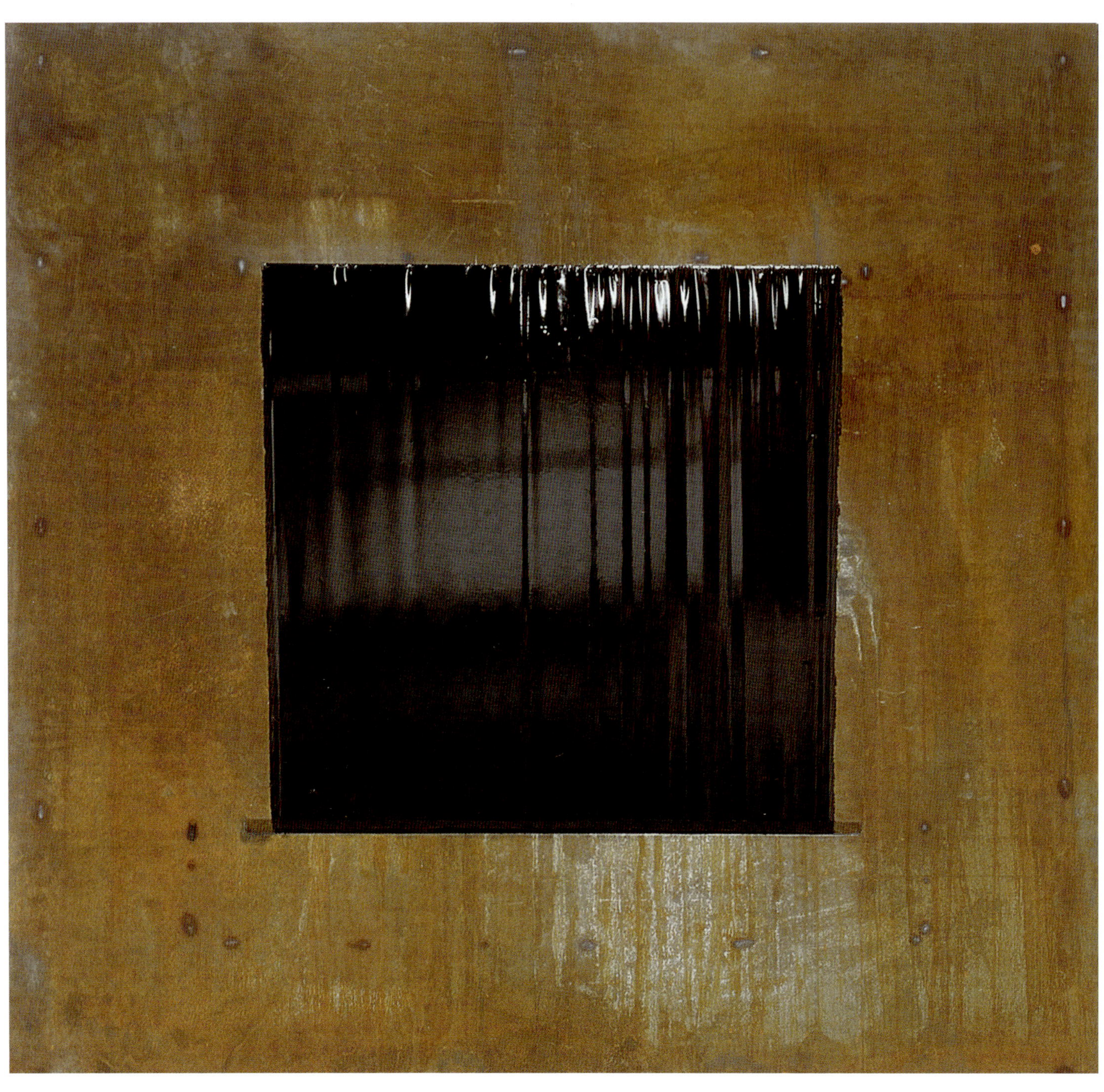

BP, *Carré Noir*, 1993. Steel, electric pump, used motor oil, 150 × 150 × 15 cm. Inv. GR5-L04
BP, *Black/Gold*, 2006. Brass, electric pump, used motor oil, 44 × 44 × 6 cm. Inv. GR5-L18

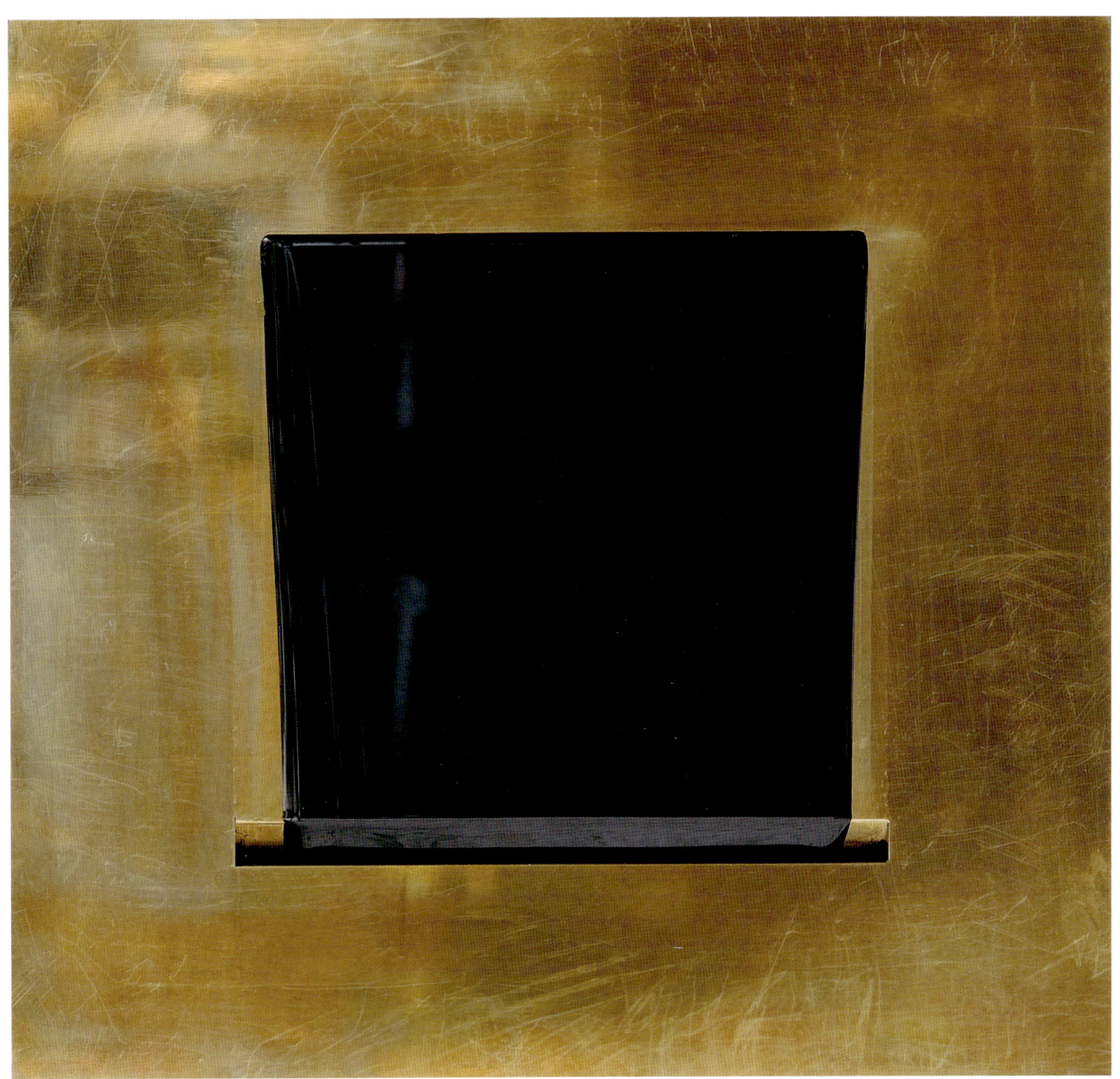

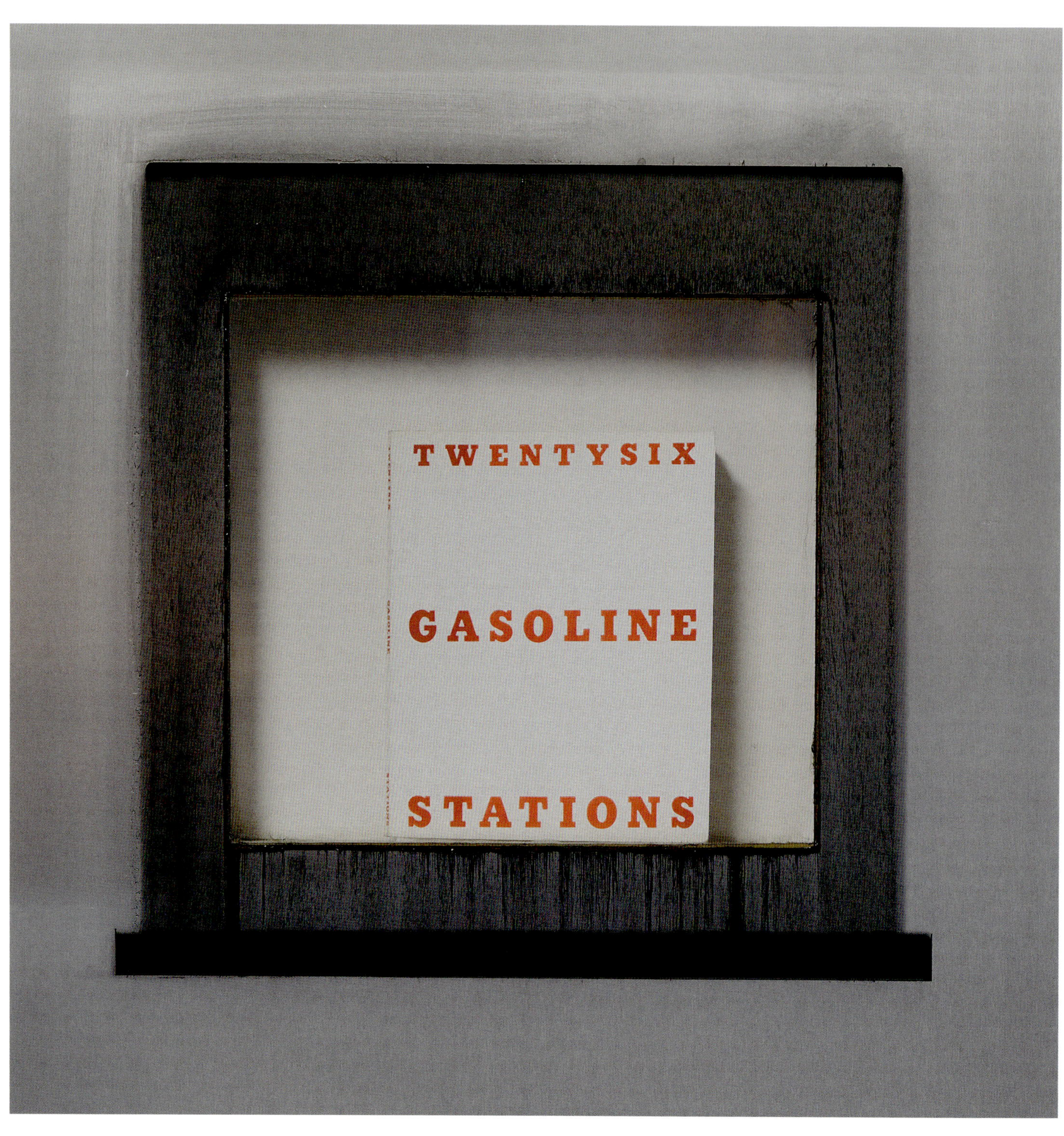

BP, *Twentysix Gasoline Stations*, 2008. Ed Ruscha, *Twentysix Gasoline Stations* book, stainless steel, electric pump, oil change, 56 × 56 cm. Inv. 3_31_00128

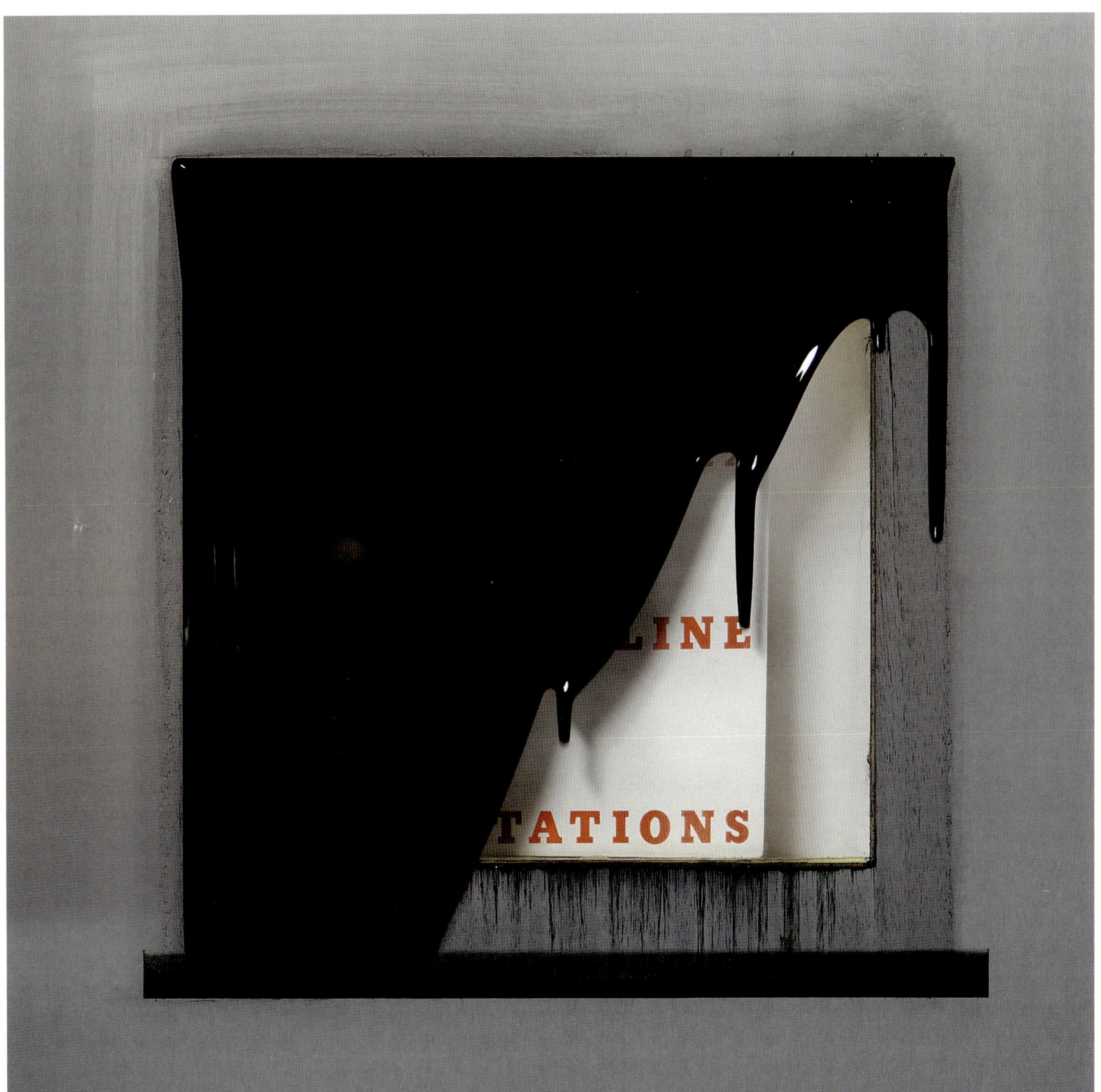
LINE
TATIONS

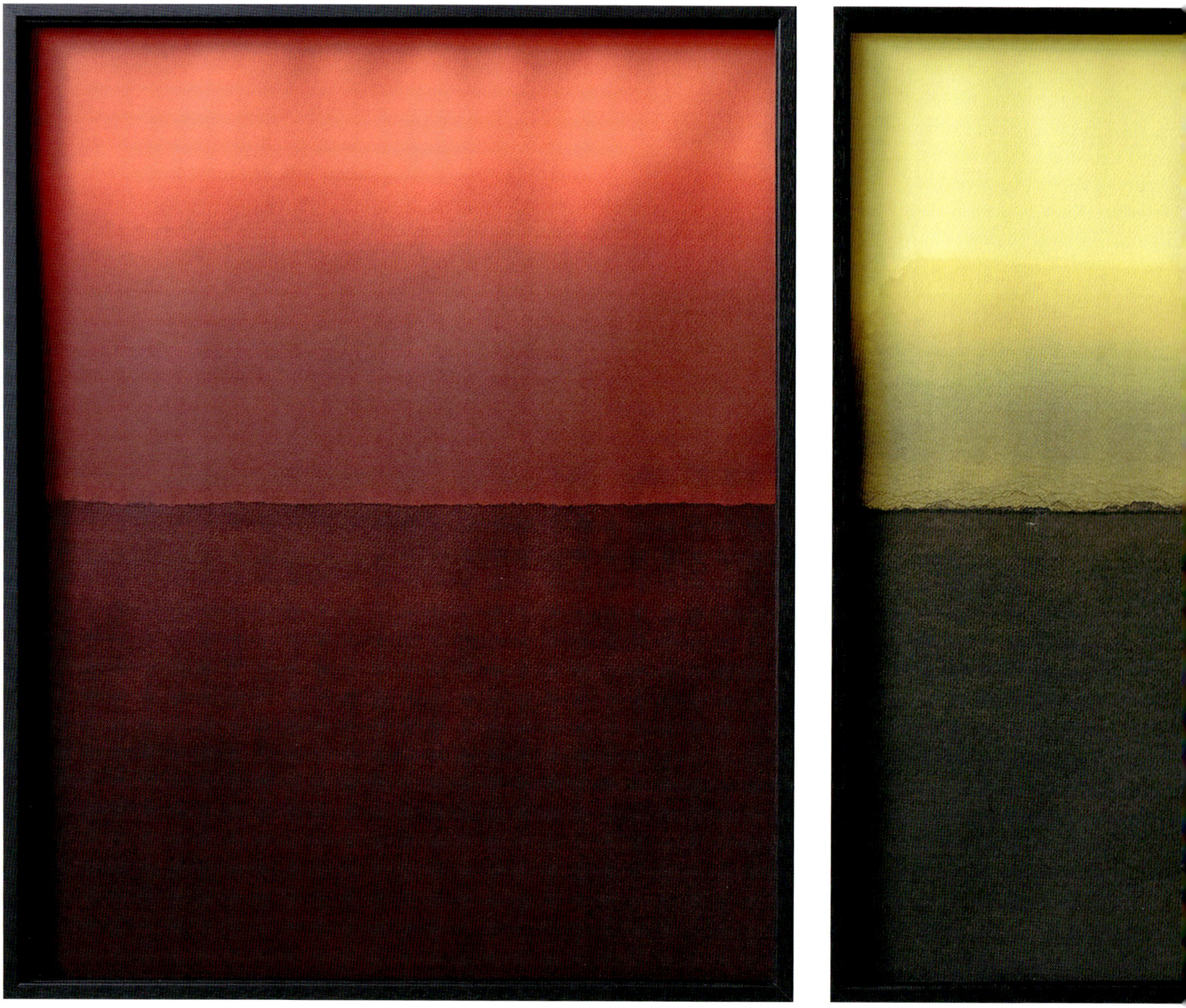

Renaud Layrac, *Horizon*, 2016. Motor oil on colored paper, 67 × 52 cm each. Inv. GR5-L10

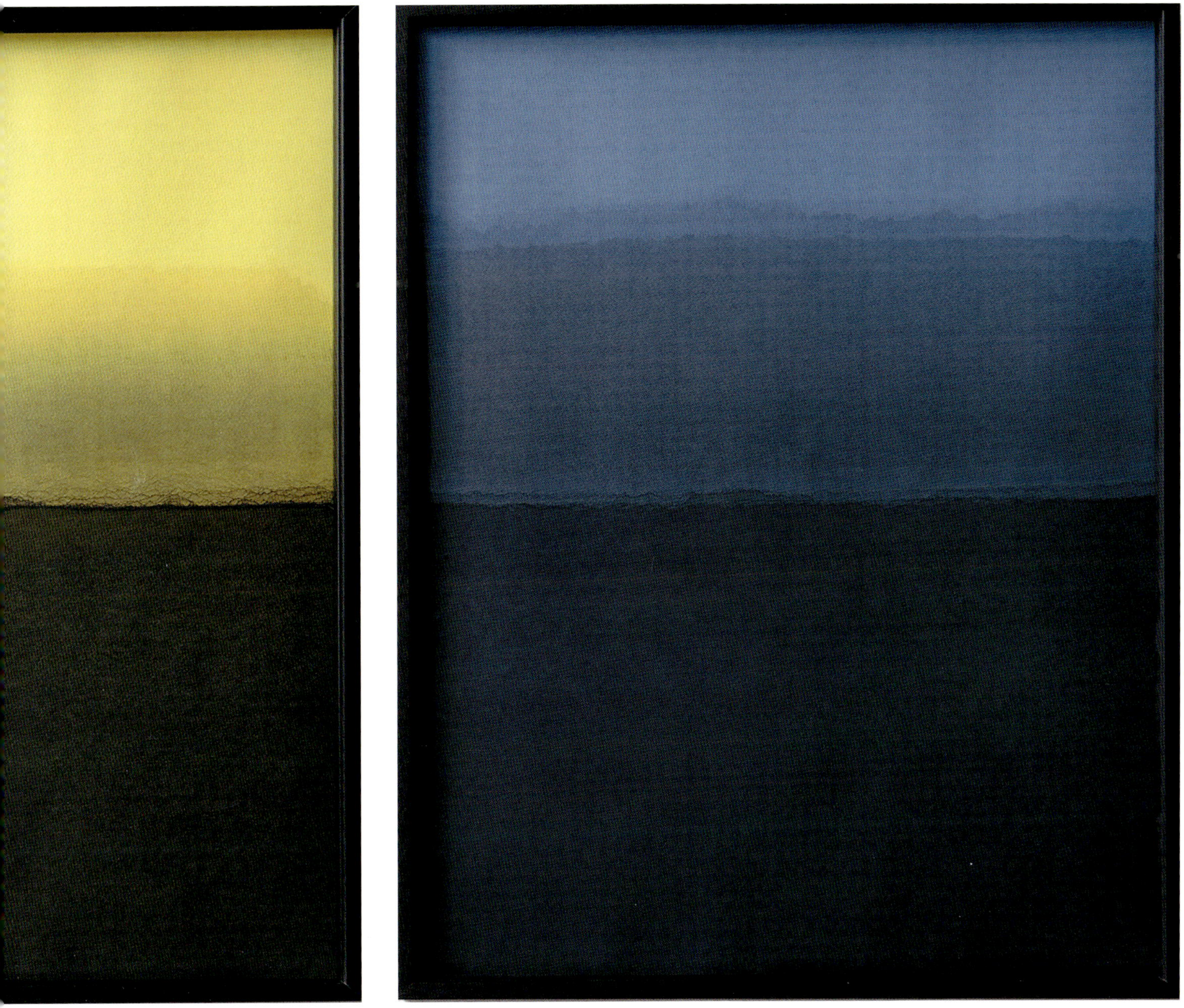

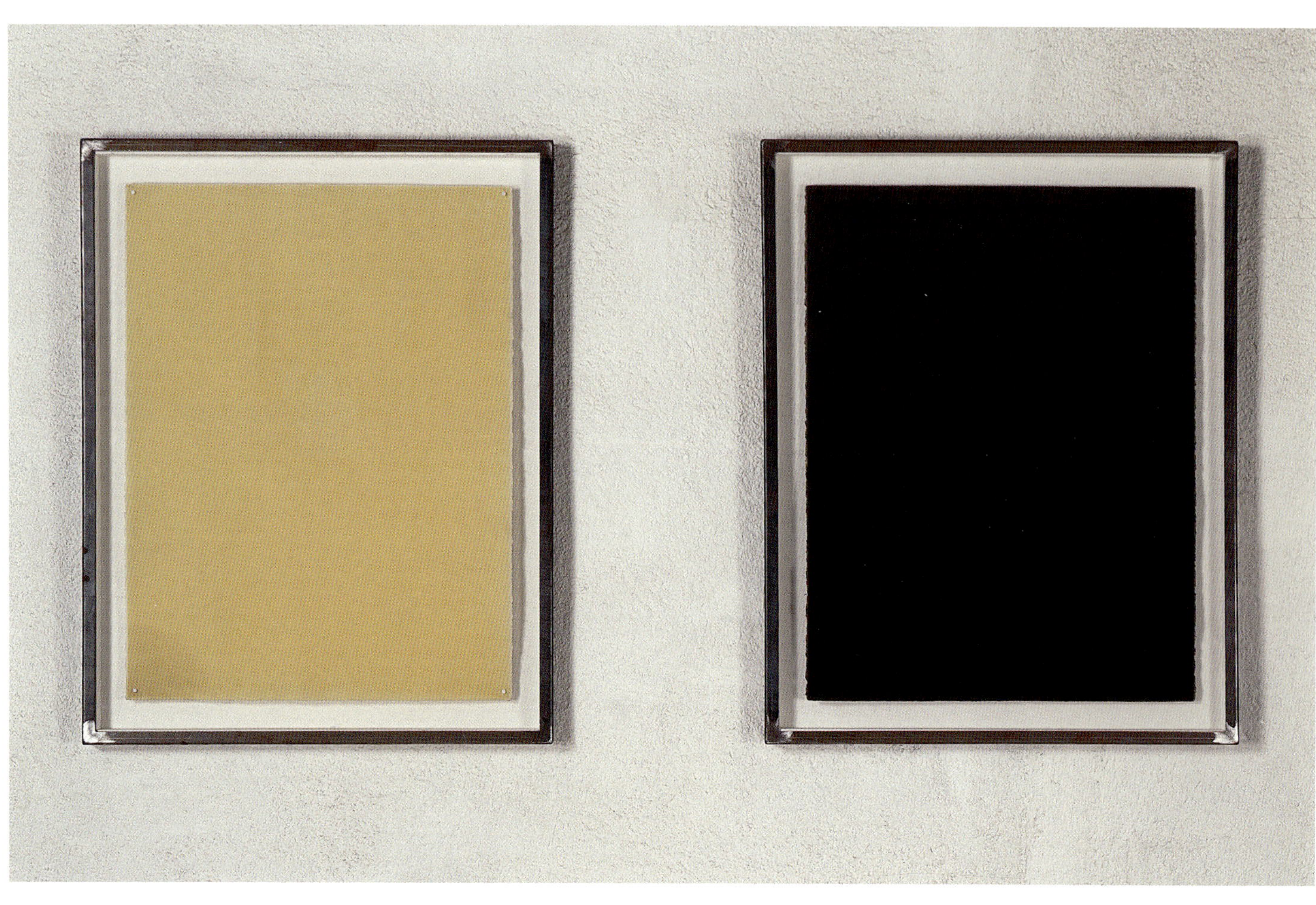

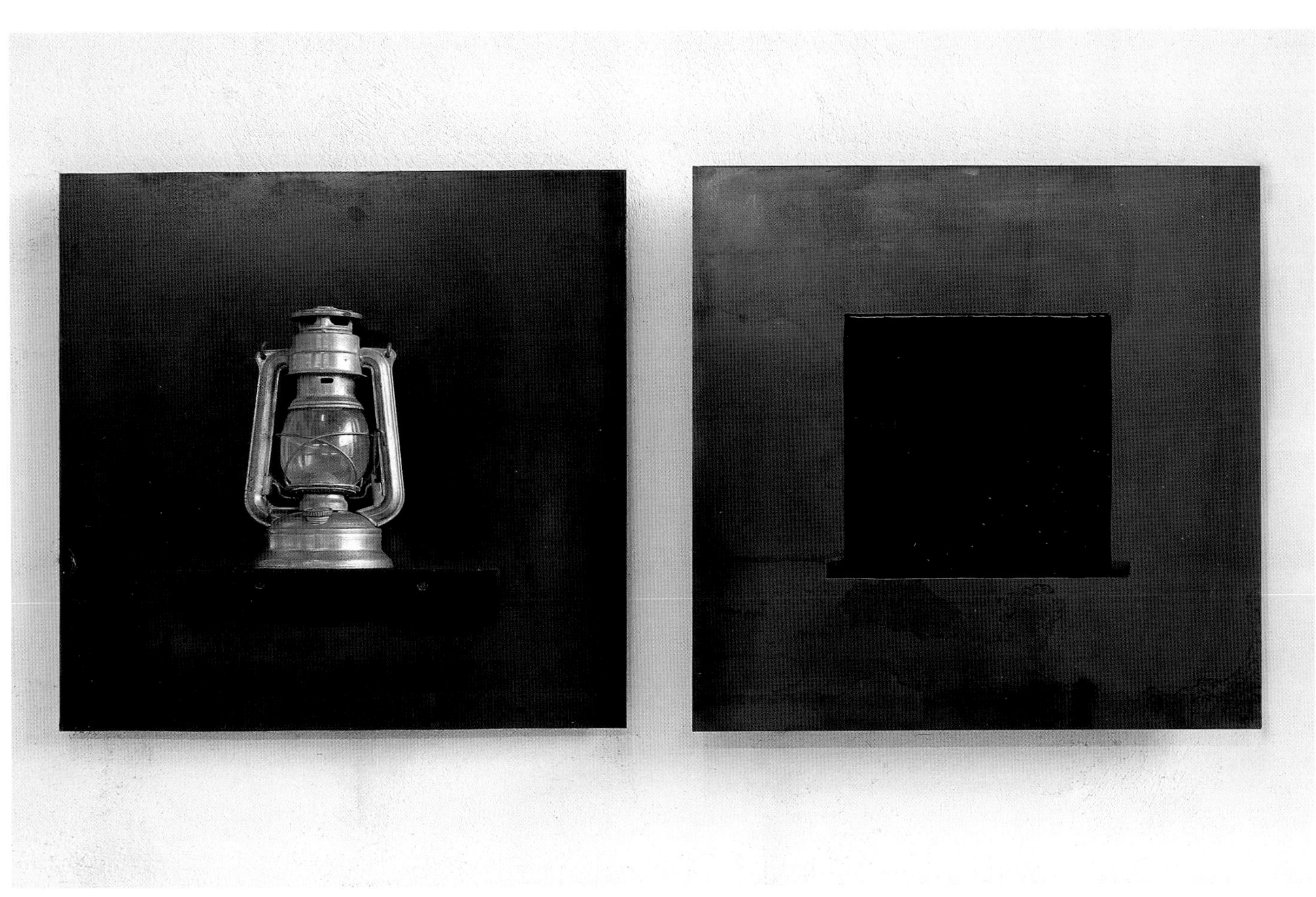

BP, *Untitled*, 1986. Motor oil on Arches papers, 88 × 68 cm each. Inv. GR5-L19
BP, *Untitled*, 1990. Steel, kerosene lamp, electric pump, waste motor oil, 55 × 55 × 10 cm each. Inv. 3_31_00124_A and 3_31_00124_B

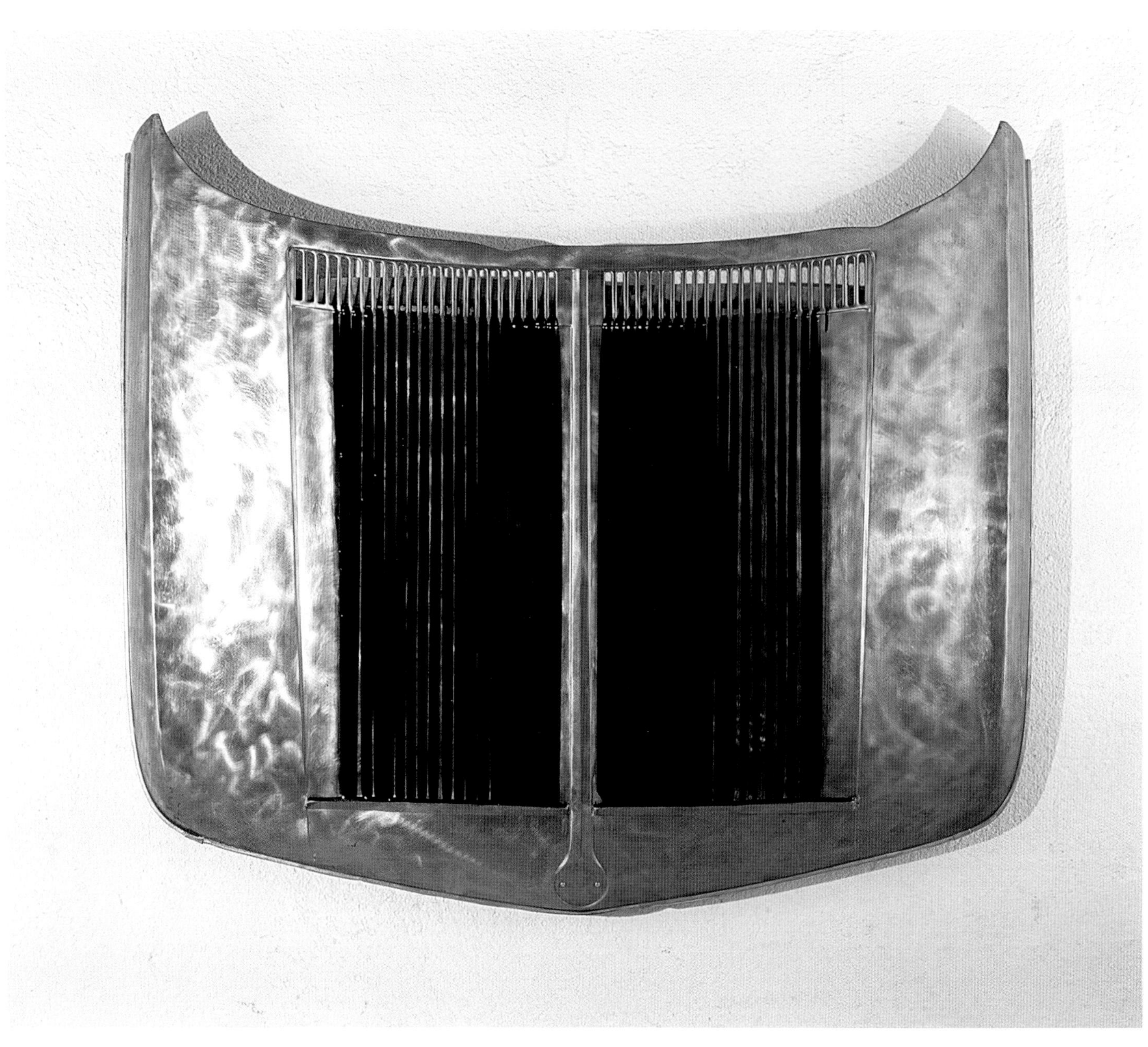

BP, *Untitled*, 1988. Car hood, used motor oil , electric pump, 135 × 153 × 15 cm. Inv. BP18
BP, *Simulator*, 1997. Aluminum, electric pump, used motor oil, 160 × 250 × 82 cm. Inv. GR5-L24

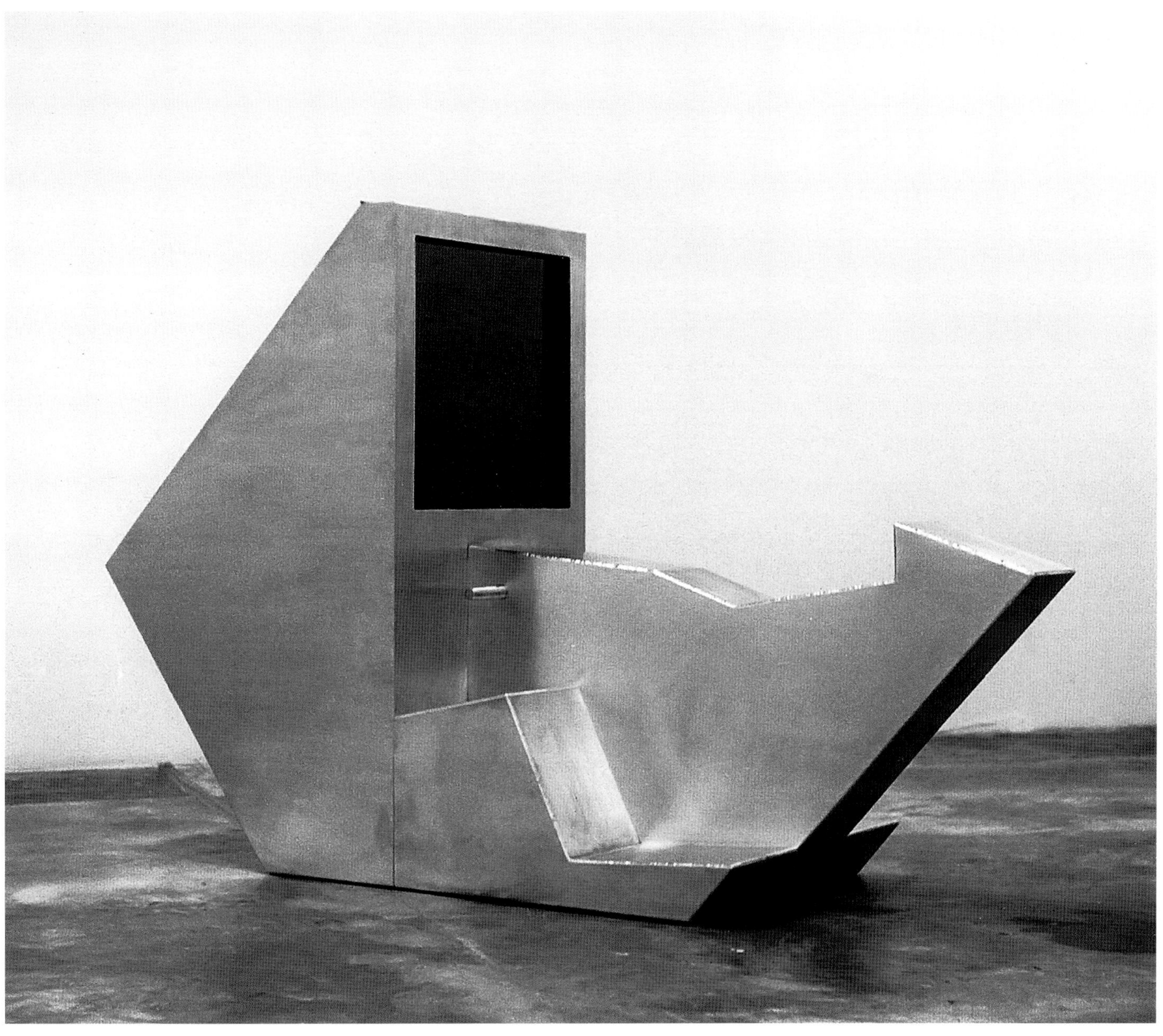

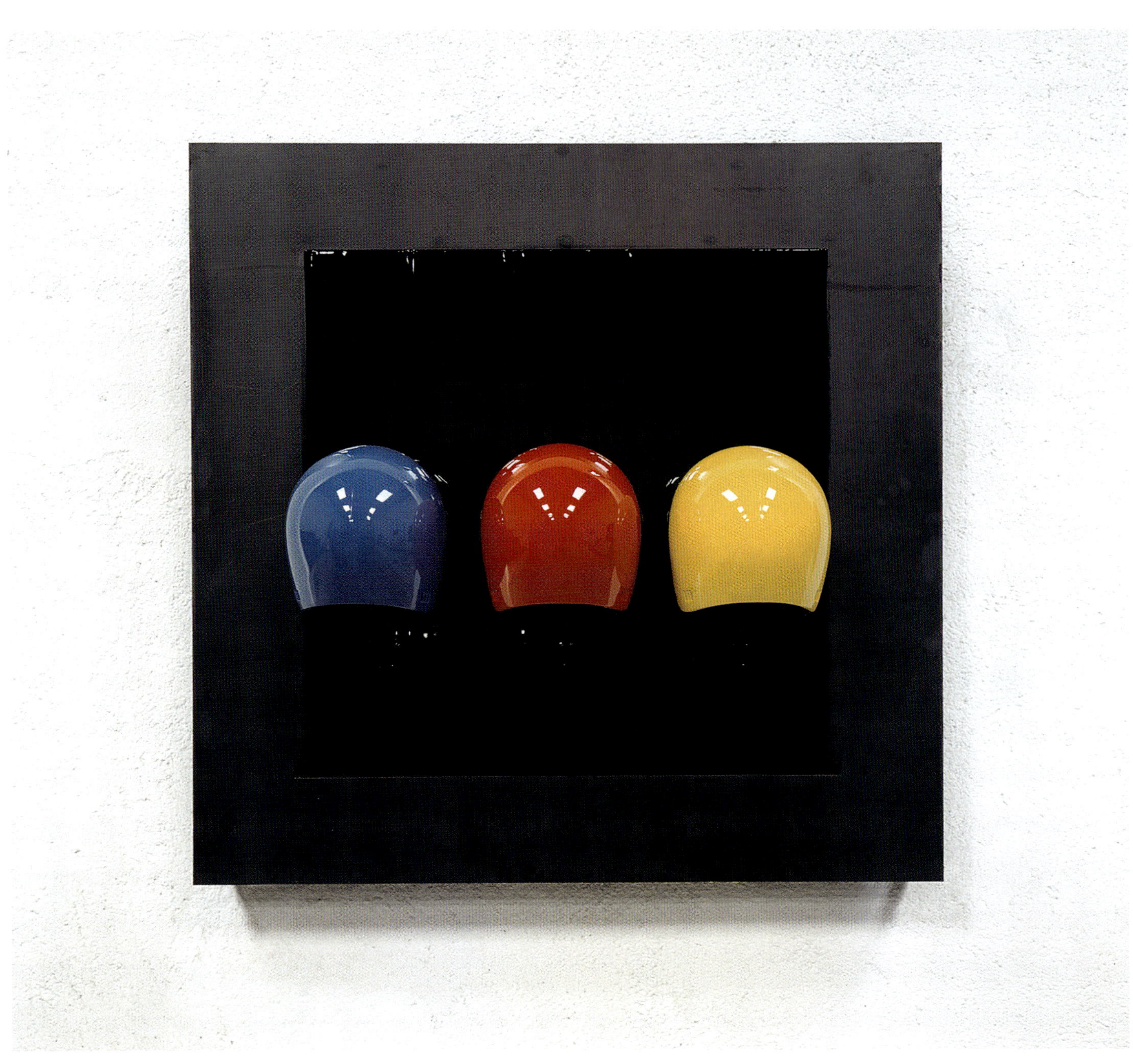

BP, *Sportsmen*, 1993. Steel, full-face helmets, electric pump, used motor oil, 125 × 125 × 50 cm. Inv. GR5-L05
BP, *Red, Yellow, Blue*, 1993. Lacquered steel, electric pump, used motor oil, 60 × 60 × 8 cm each. Inv. GR5-L06

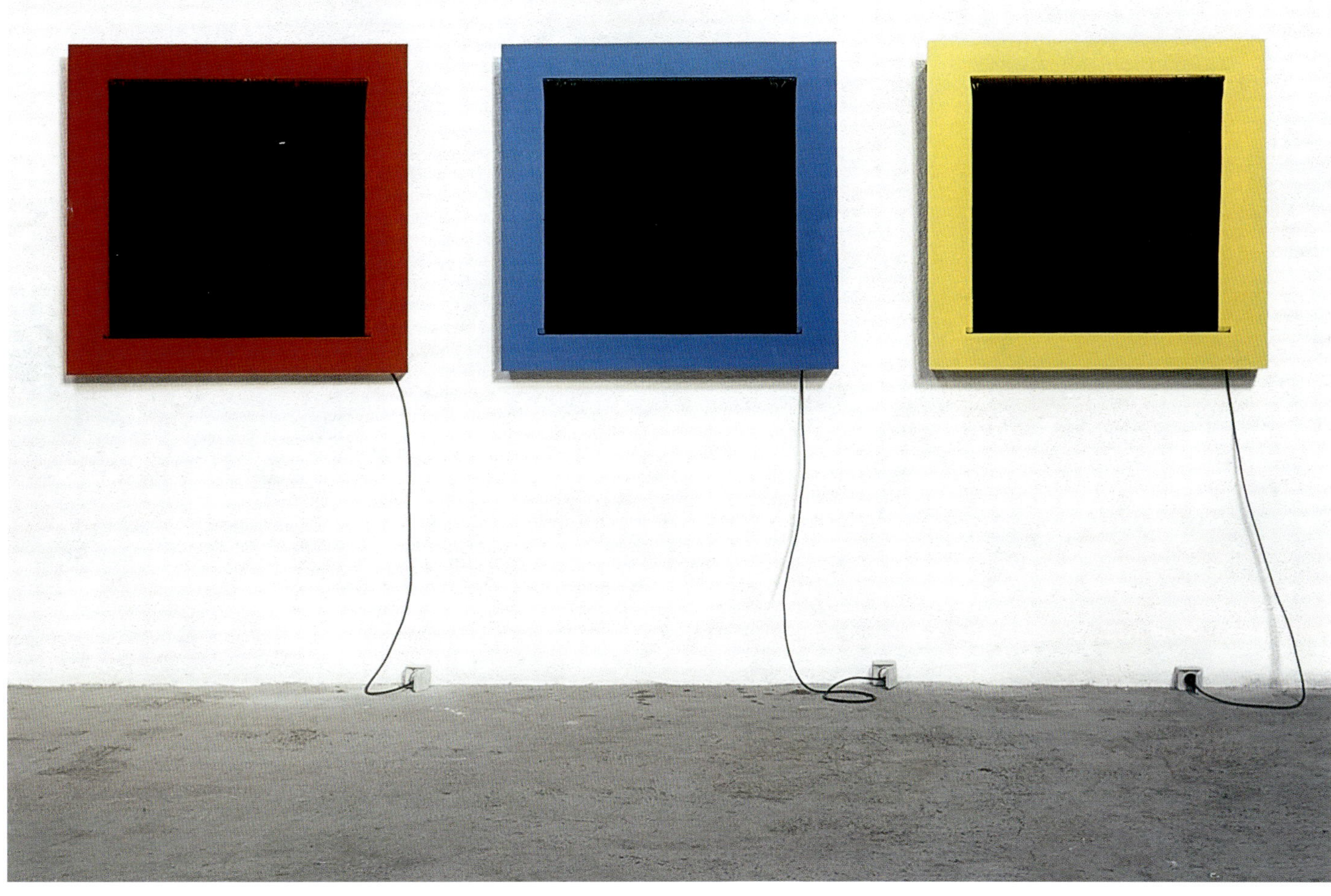

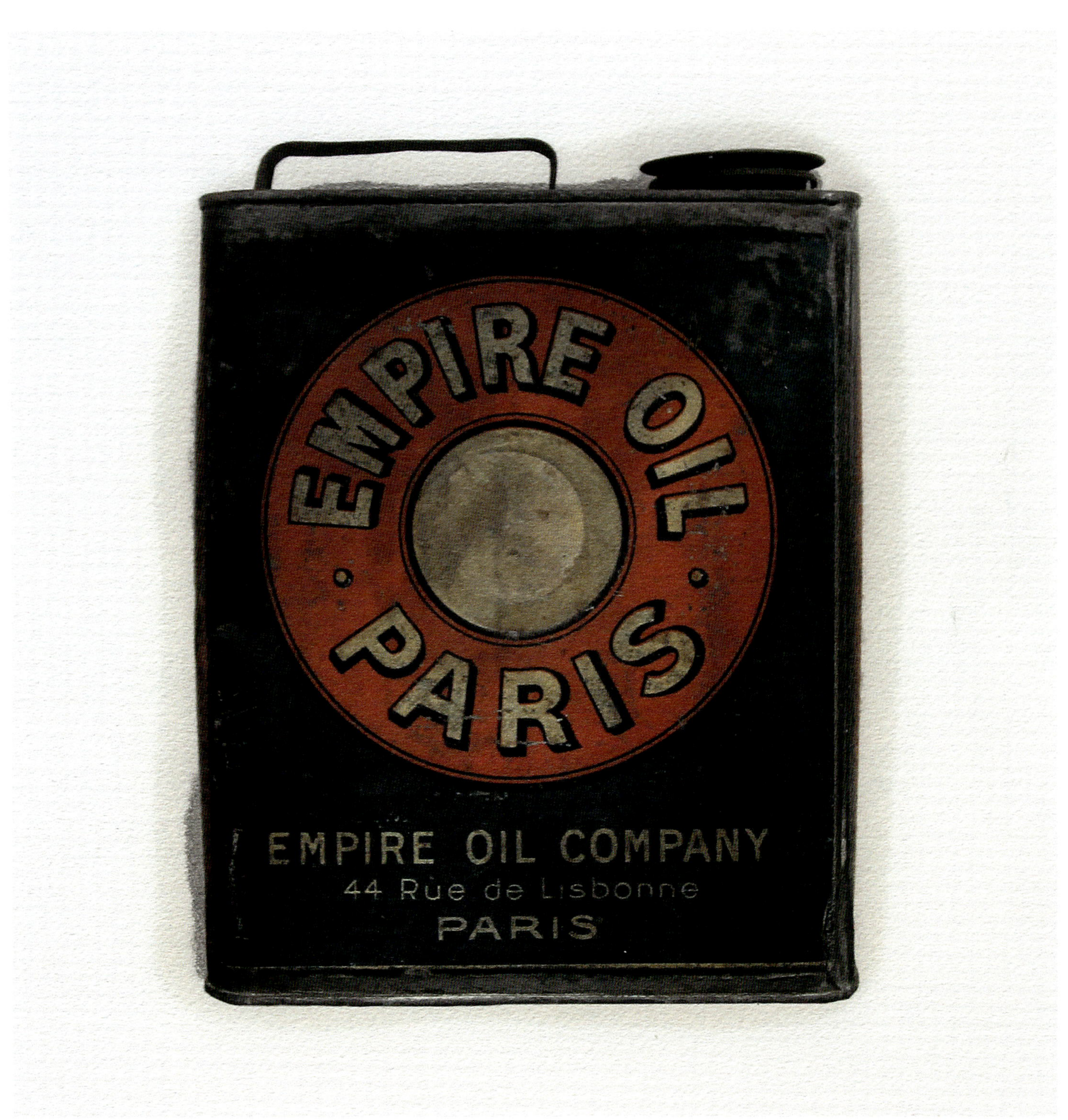

BP, *Empire Oil*, 2007. Print, used motor oil on Arches paper, 45 × 45 cm. Inv. GR5-L07
BP, *Untitled*, 1990–2008. Print, used motor oil on Arches paper, 45 × 45 cm each. Inv. GR5-L15

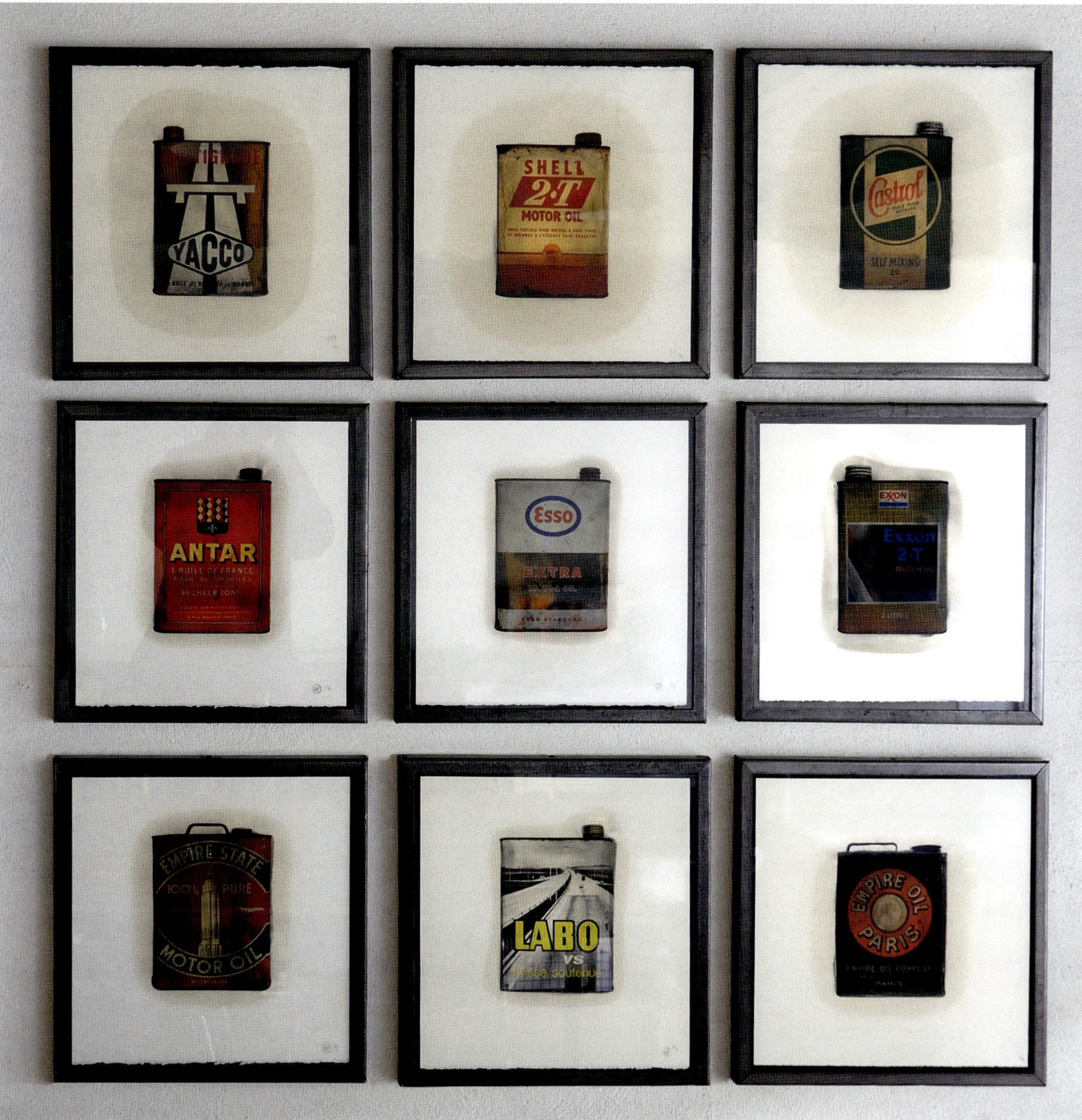
YACCO
SHELL
2-T
MOTOR OIL
Castrol
SELF MIXING
ANTAR
L'HUILE DE FRANCE
Esso
EXTRA
EXXON
Exxon
2 T
2 LITRE
EMPIRE STATE
100% PURE
MOTOR OIL
LABO
vs
EMPIRE OIL
PARIS

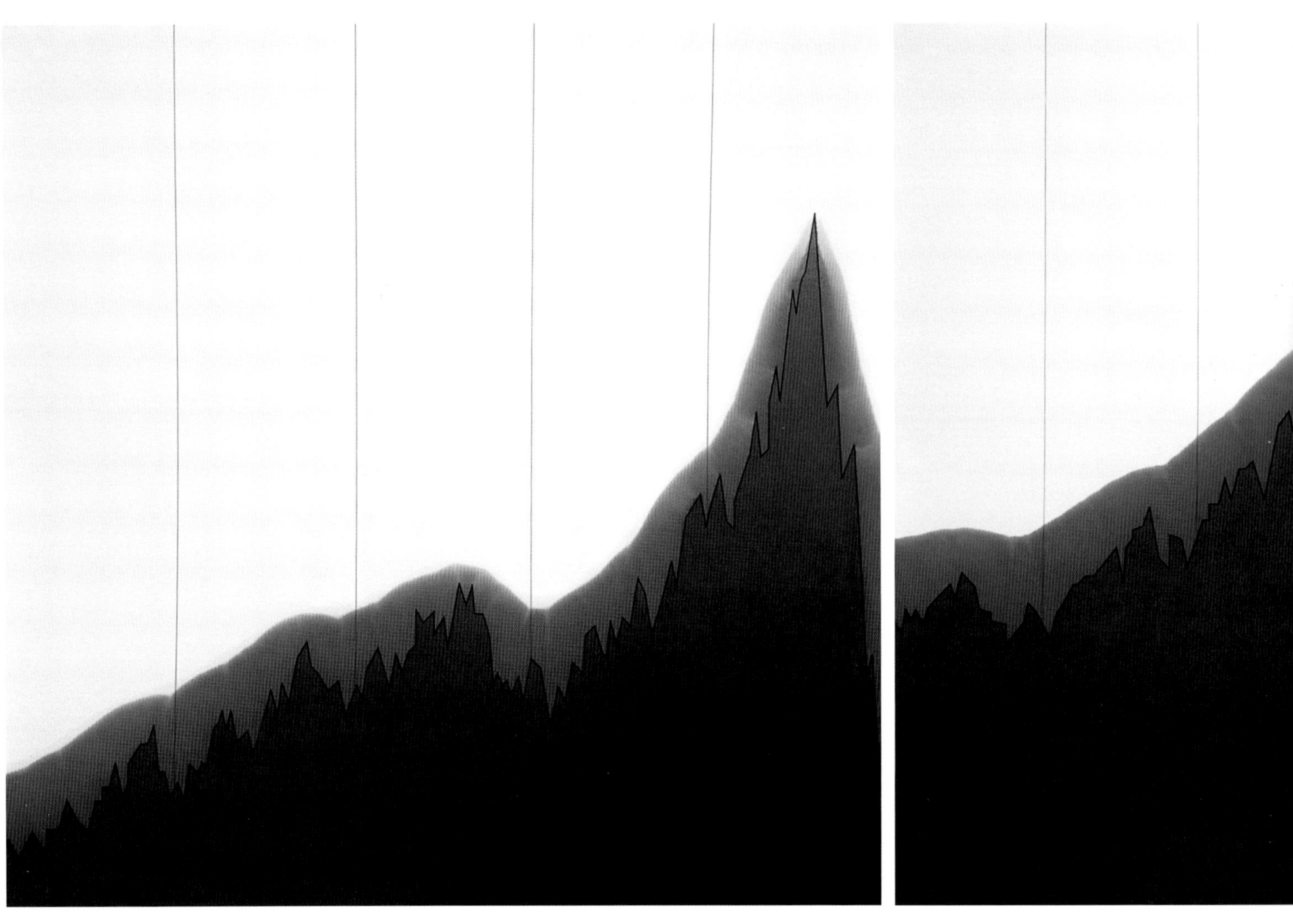

BP, *Up and Down X3*, 2008. Print, used motor oil on Arches paper, 89 × 89 cm each. Inv. GR5-L14

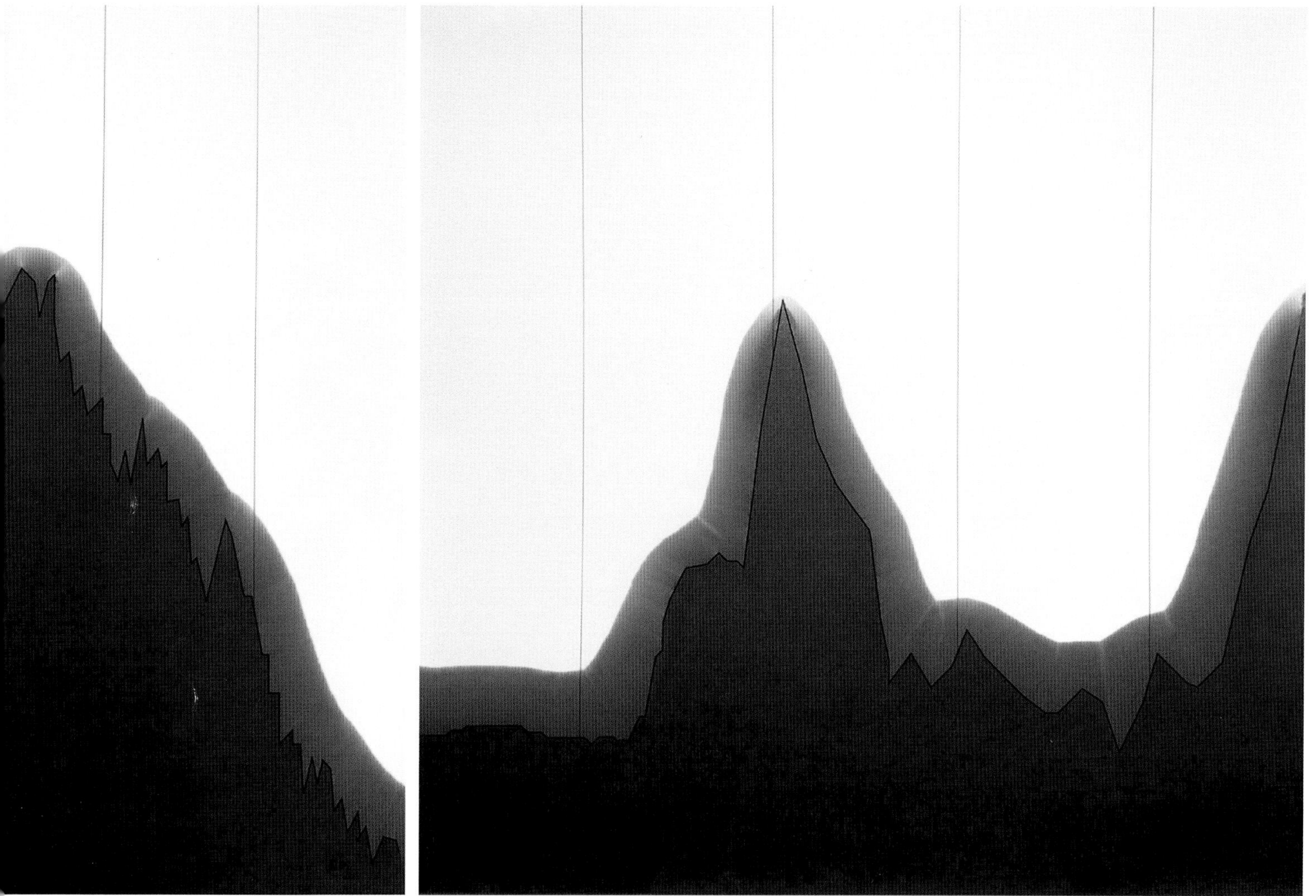

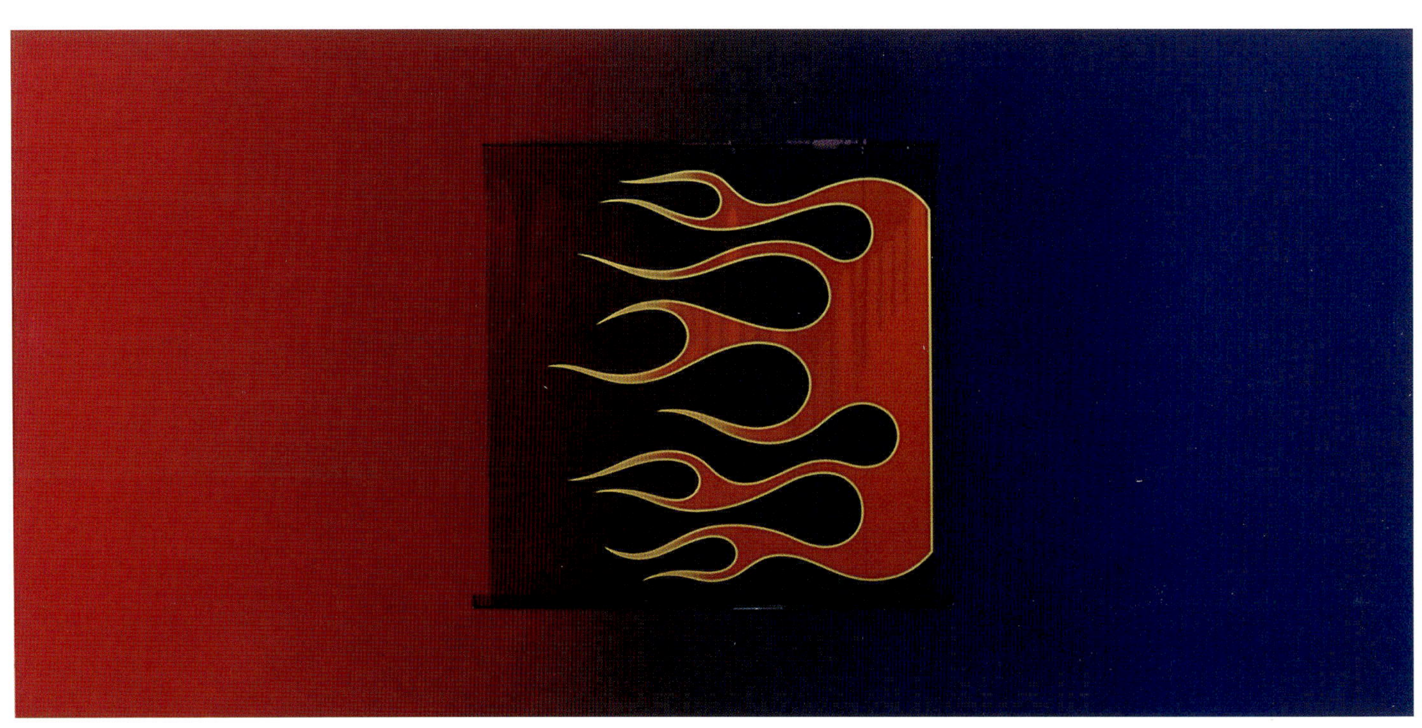

BP, *Untitled*, 1997. Lacquered steel, electric pump, used motor oil, 124 × 244 × 22 cm. Inv. GR5-L12
BP, *Untitled*, 1997. Lacquered metal drums, electric pump, used motor oil, 204 × 81 × 81 cm. Inv. GR5-L26

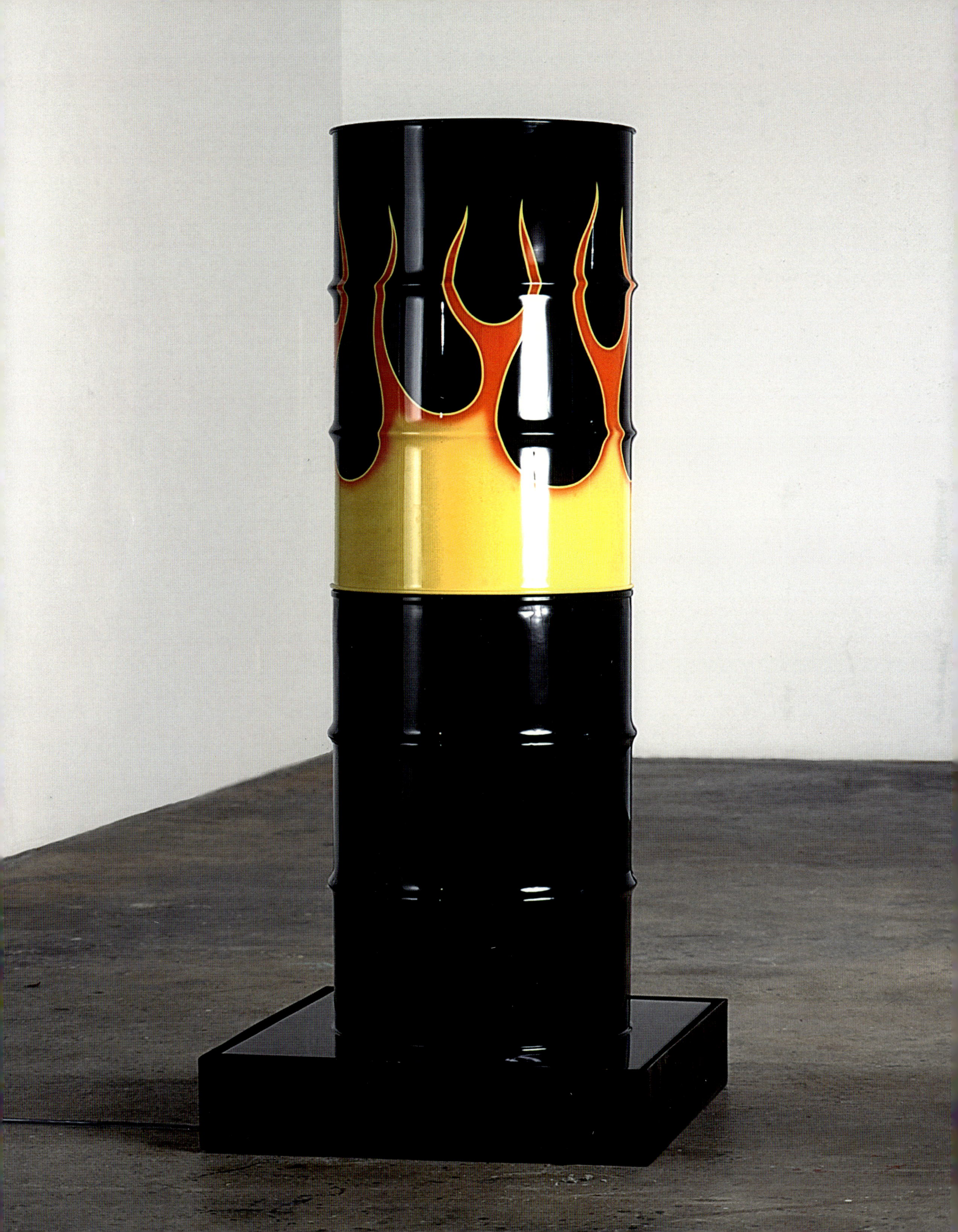

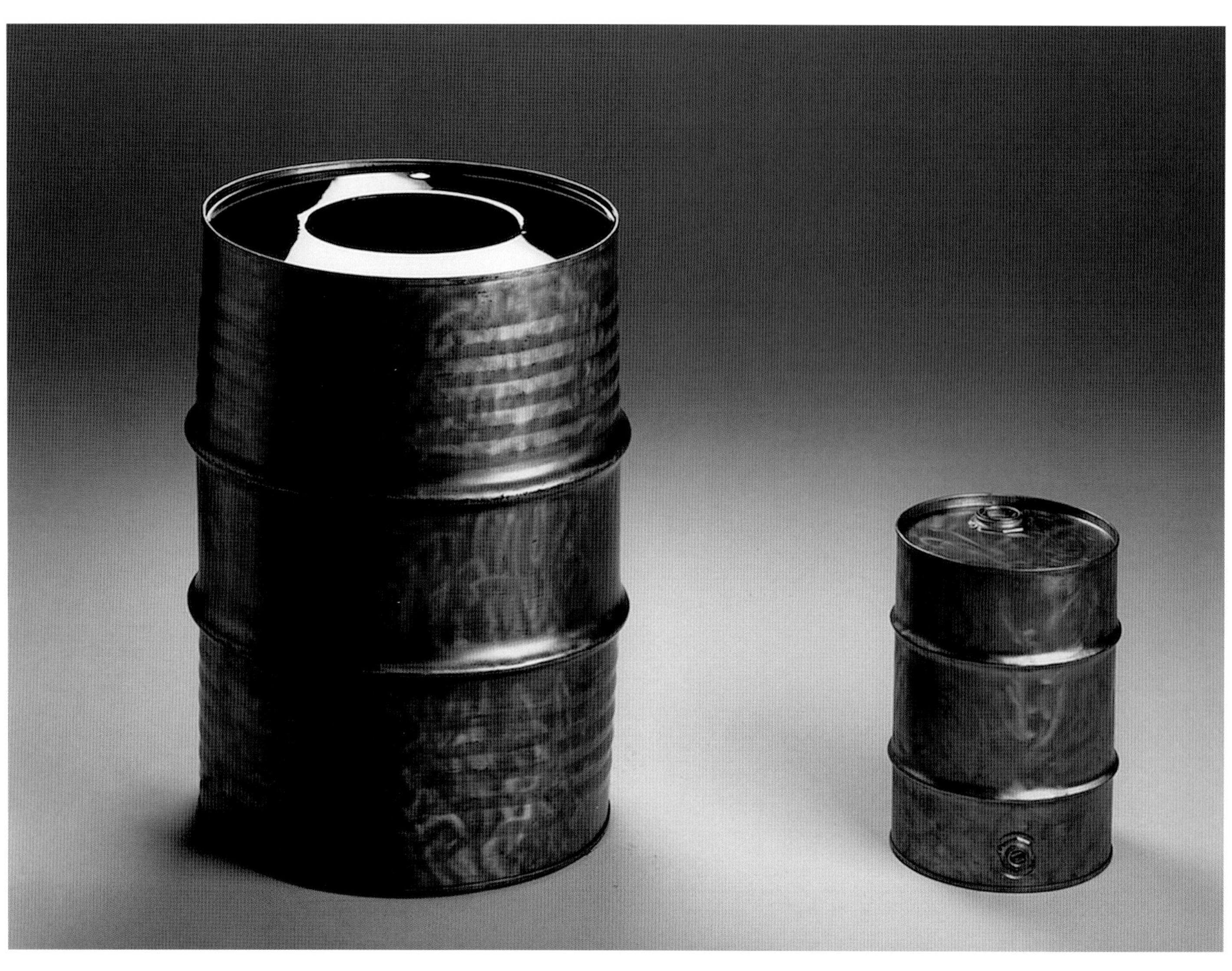

BP, *Plus Ou Moins*, 1987. Metal drums, electric pump, used motor oil, 89 × 57 cm, 45 × 31 cm. Inv. GR5-L20
BP, *Untitled*, 1987. Metal drums, steel, electric pump, used motor oil, 115 × 90 × 90 cm. Inv. GR5-L22.
Courtesy of the Centre Pompidou

Following pages
BP, *Untitled*, 1988. Steel, traffic signs, electric pump, used motor oil, 250 × 50 × 15 cm. Inv. GR5-L01
BP, *Colonne*, 1987. Metal drums, electric pump, used motor oil, 250 × 57 × 57 cm. Inv. GR5-L21

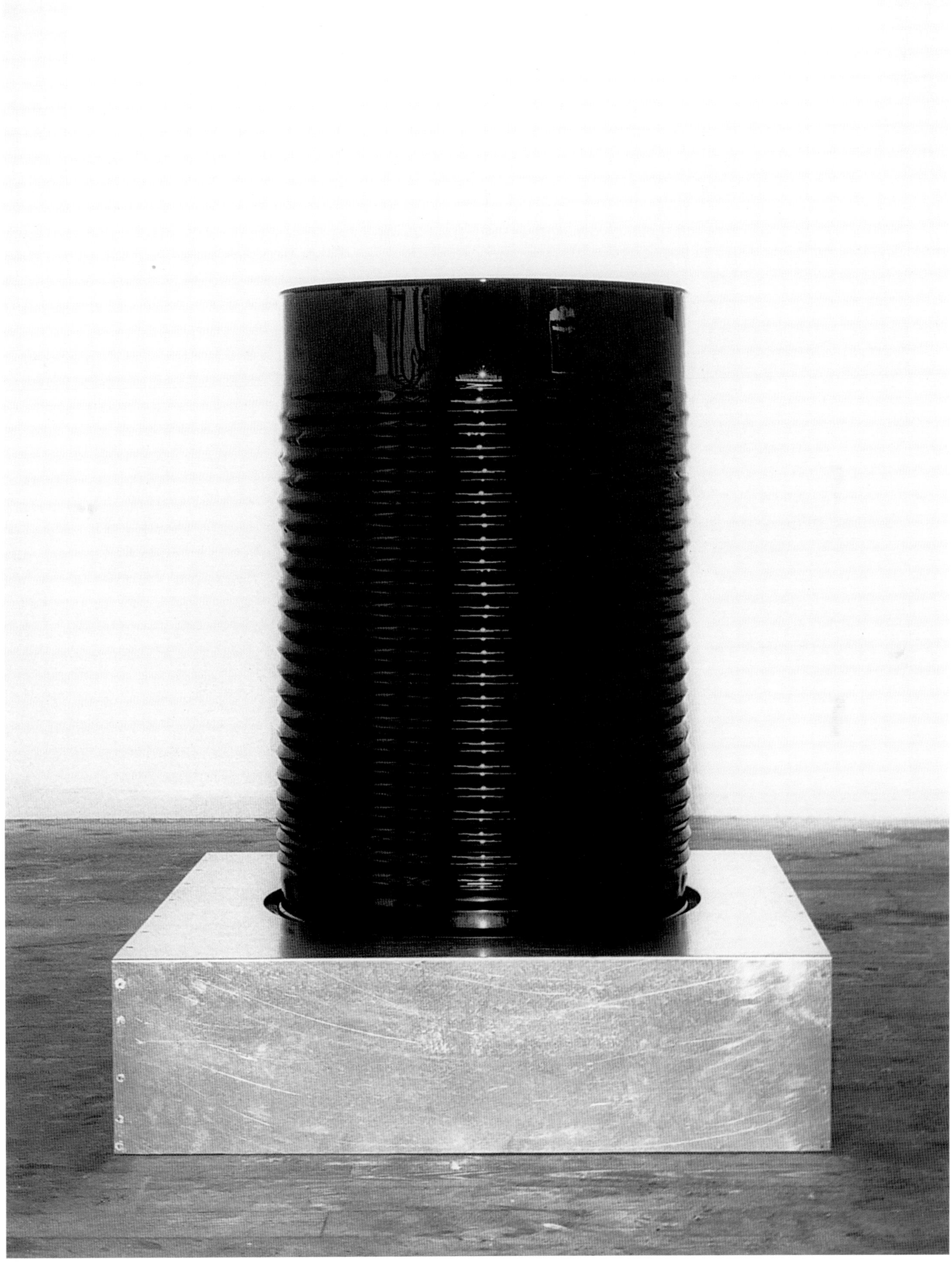

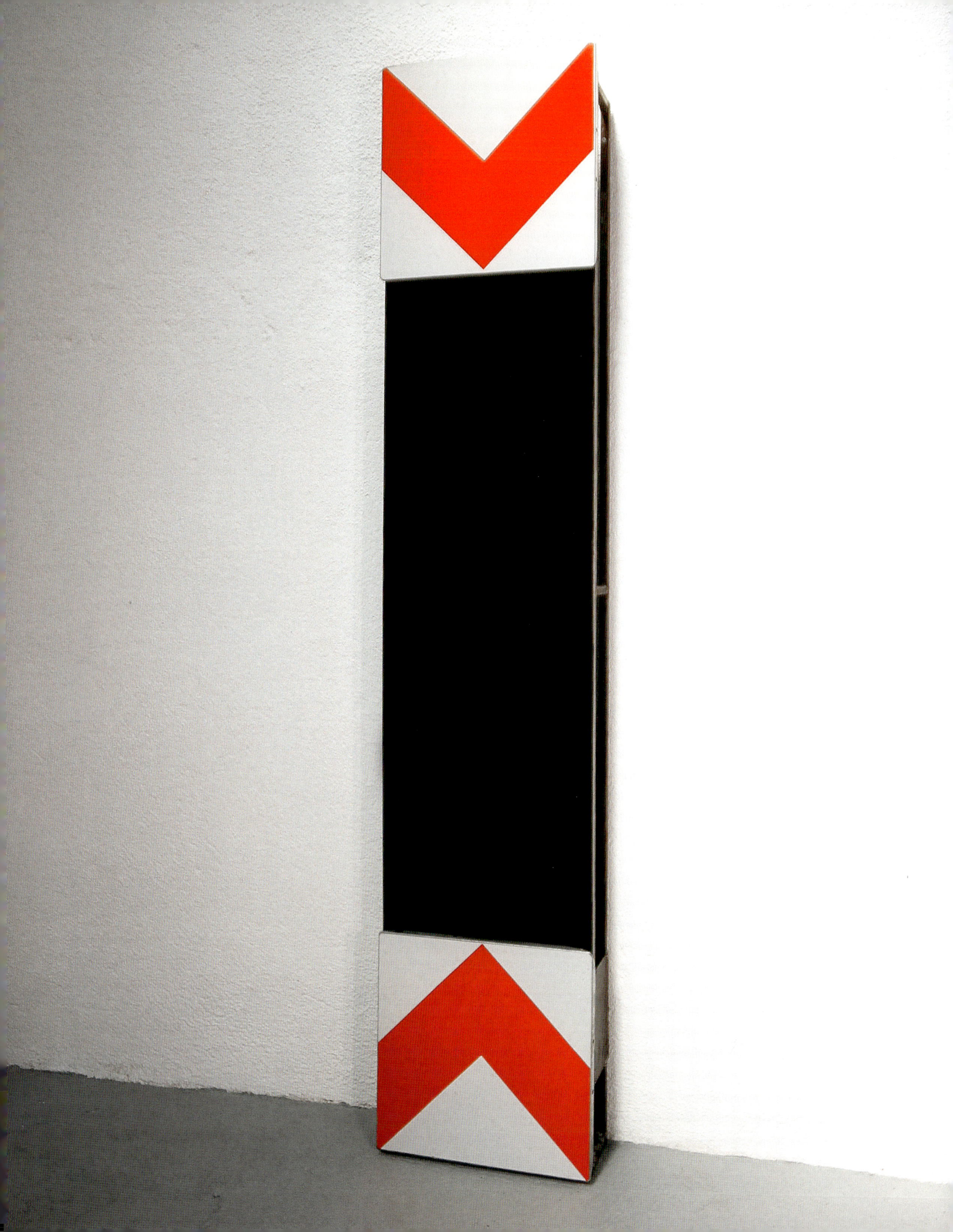

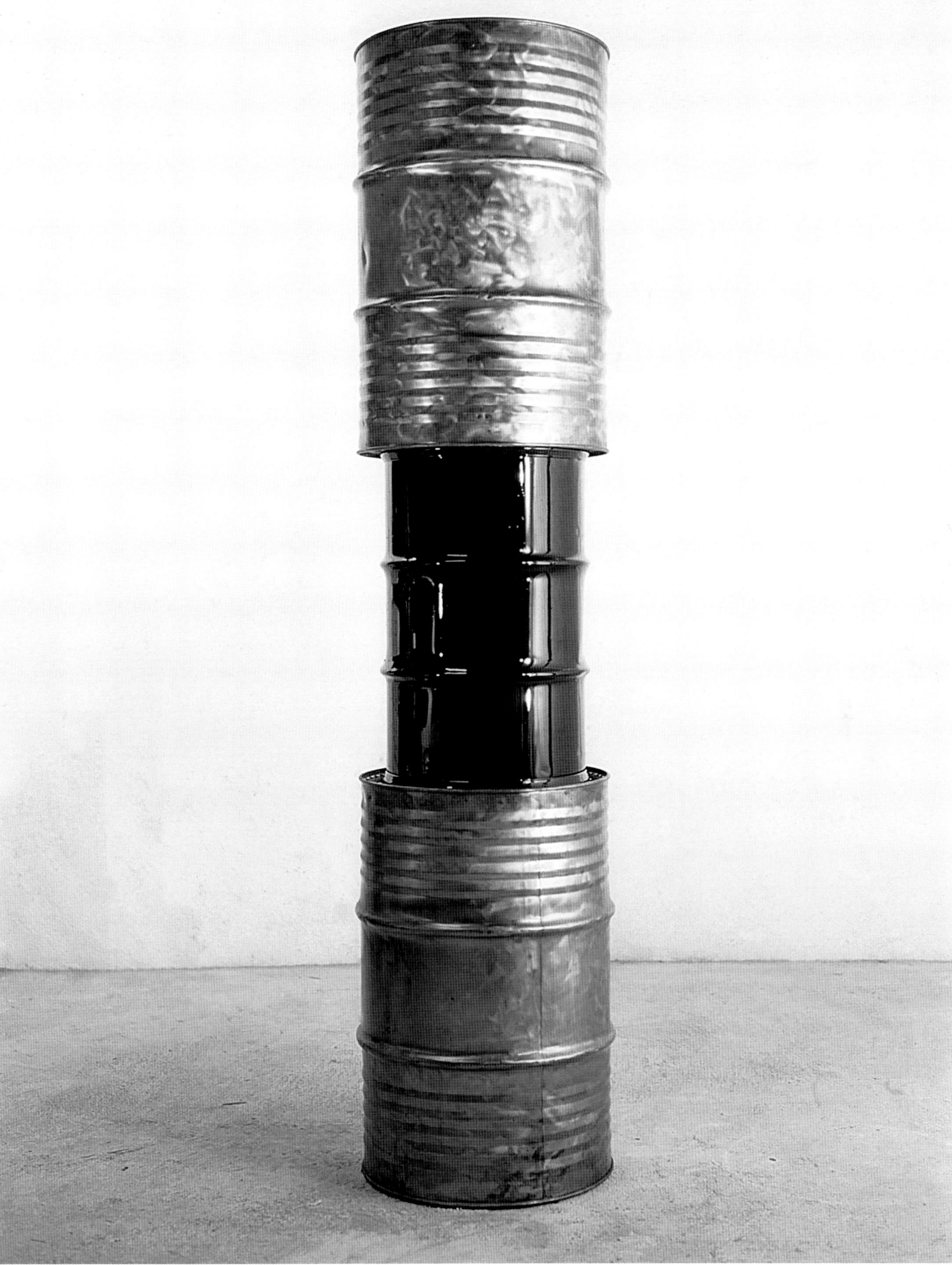

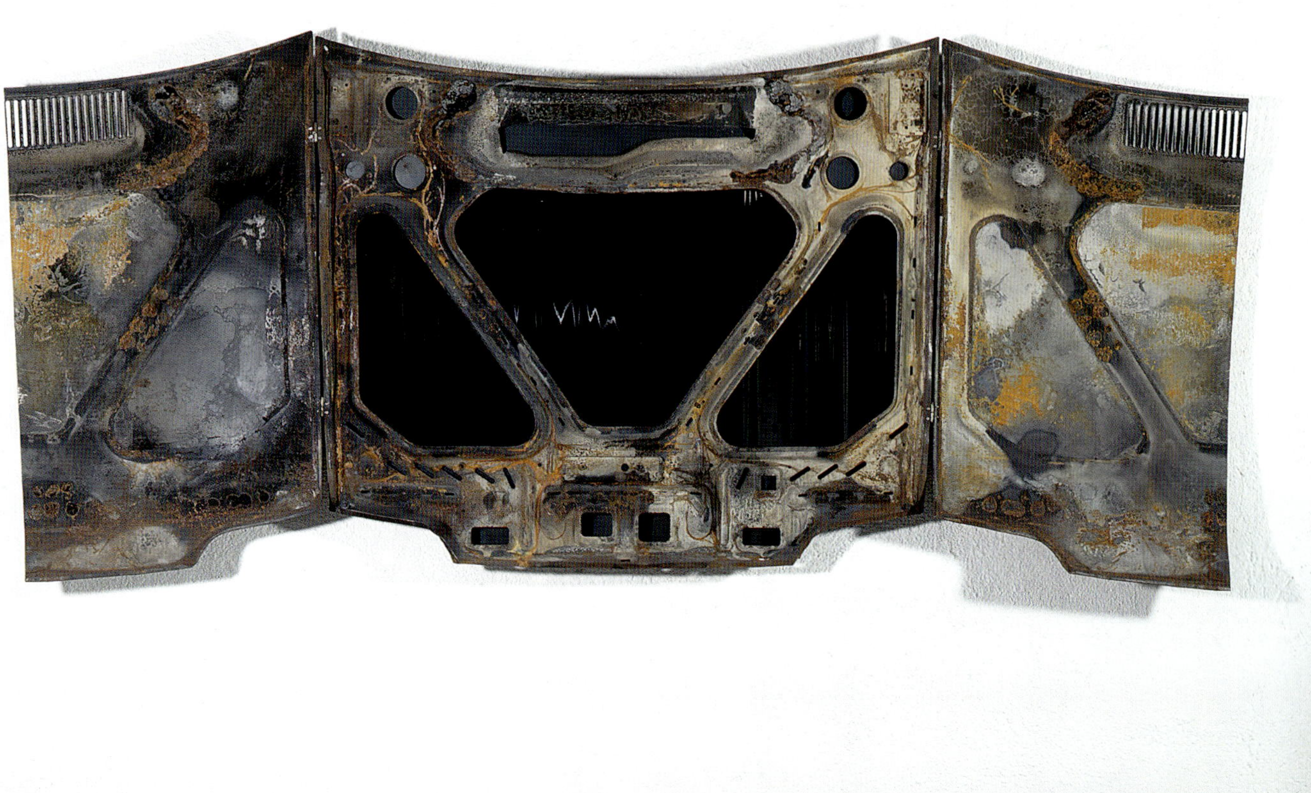

BP, *Triptyque*, 1993. Steel, electric pump, used motor oil, 117 × 258 × 12 cm. Inv. GR5-L03

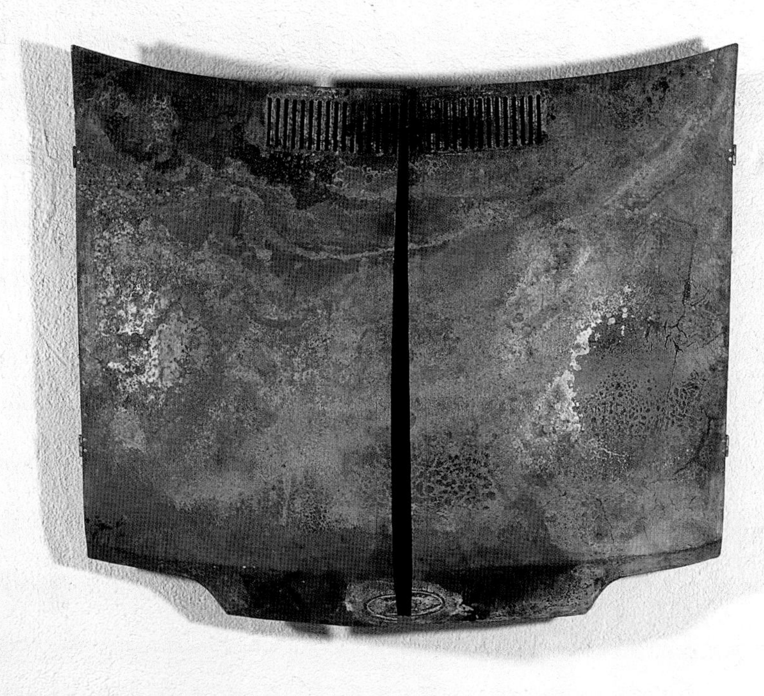

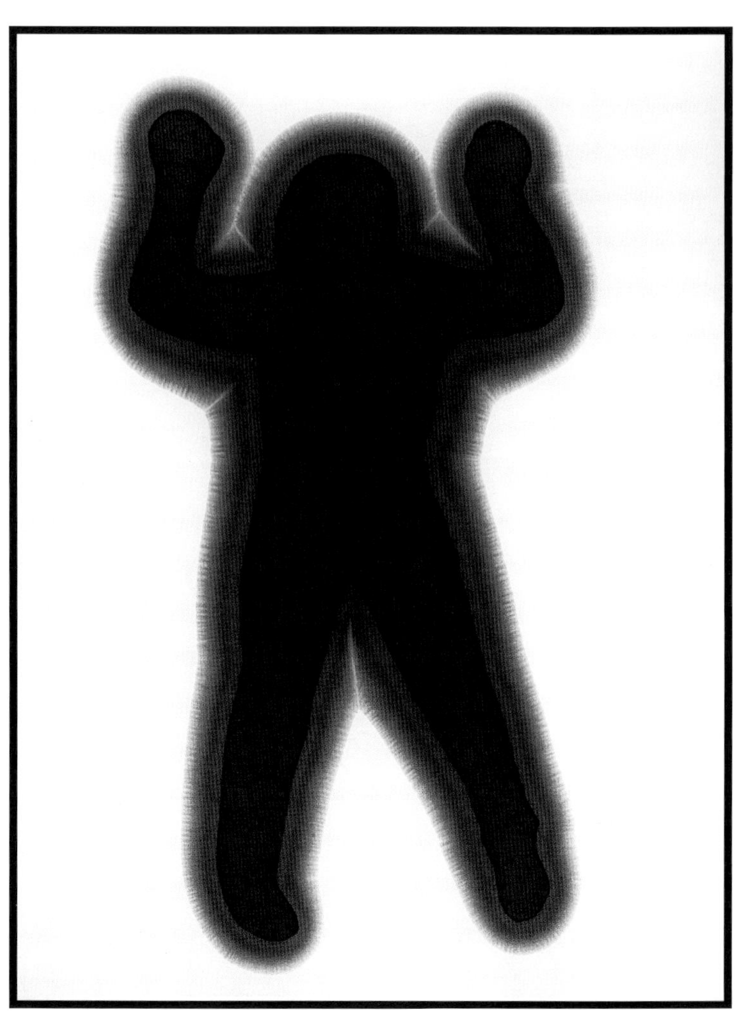

BP, *Anonyme #2*, 1996. Graphite and used motor oil on Arches paper, steel frame, 234 × 154 × 3 cm. Inv. D419
BP, *Anonyme #3*, 1996. Graphite and used motor oil on Arches paper, steel frame, 234 × 154 × 3 cm. Inv. D420
BP, *Anonyme #8*, 1996. Graphite and used motor oil on Arches paper, steel frame, 234 × 154 × 3 cm. Inv. GRS-L09

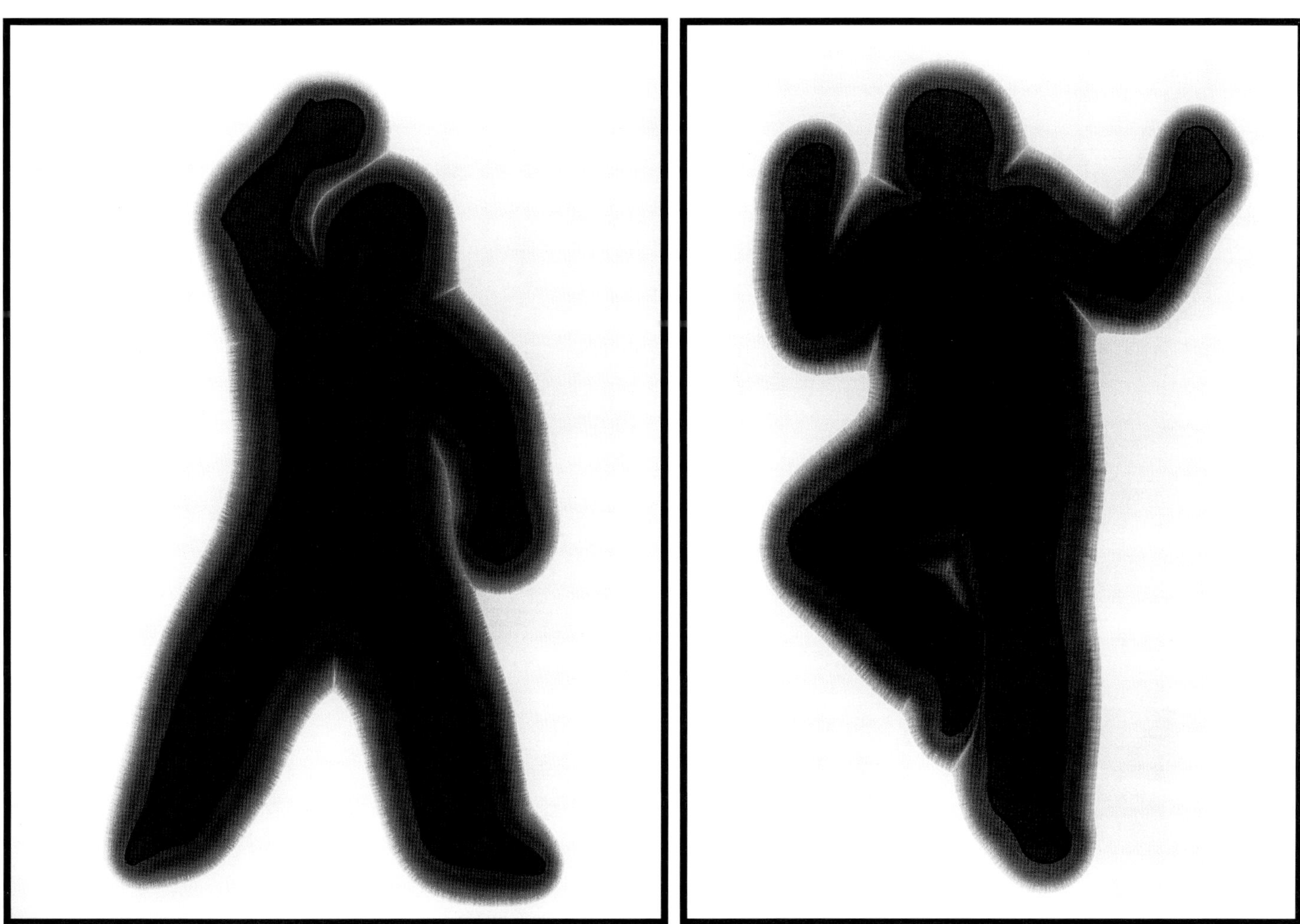

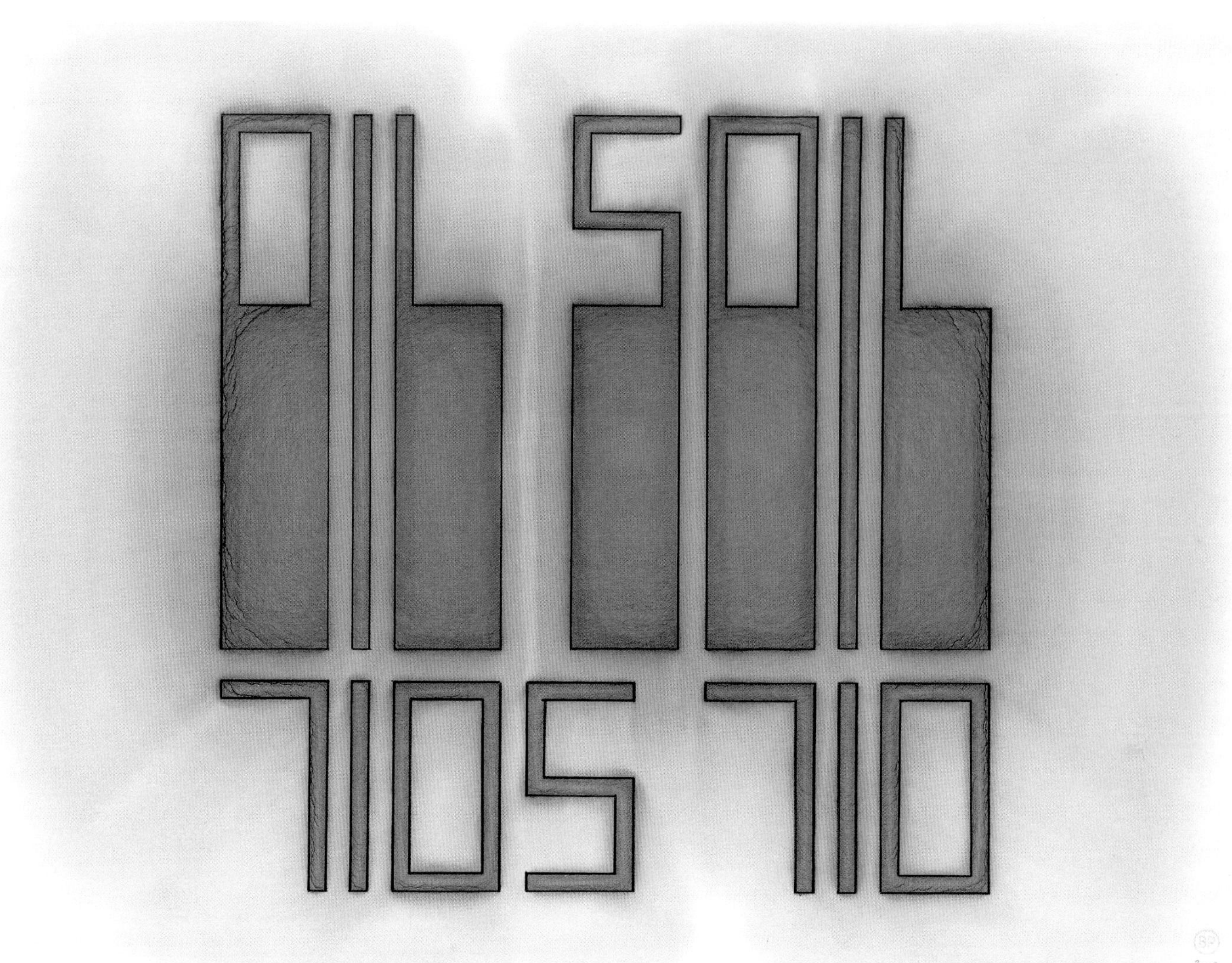

BP, *Oil Soil*, 2003. Graphite, used motor oil on Arches paper, 58 x 72 cm. Inv. GR5-L11
BP, *Unleash the Energy*, 2008. Stainless steel, electric pump, used motor oil, 135 × 135 × 12 cm. Inv. 3_31_00123

UNLEASH THE ENERGY

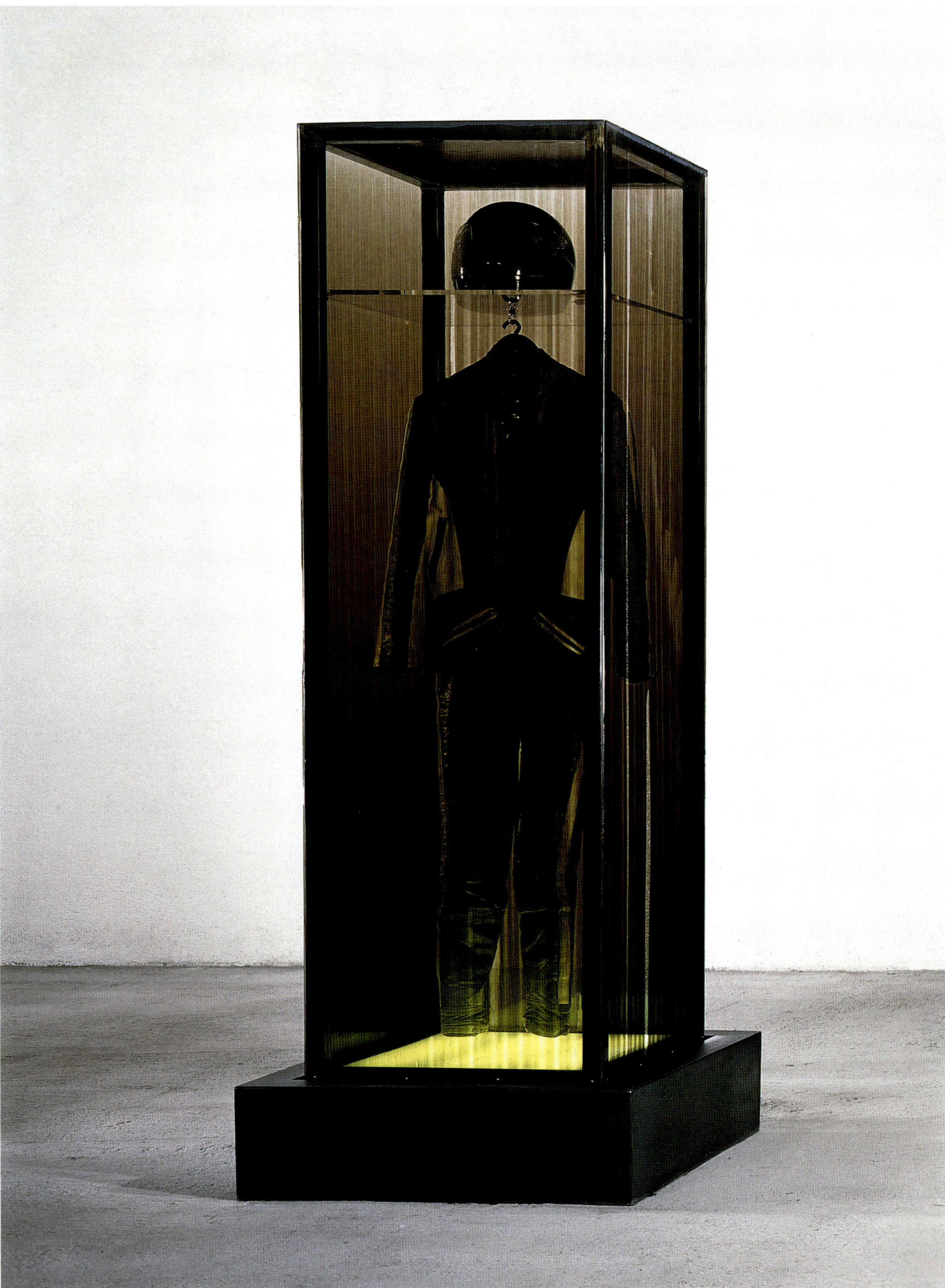

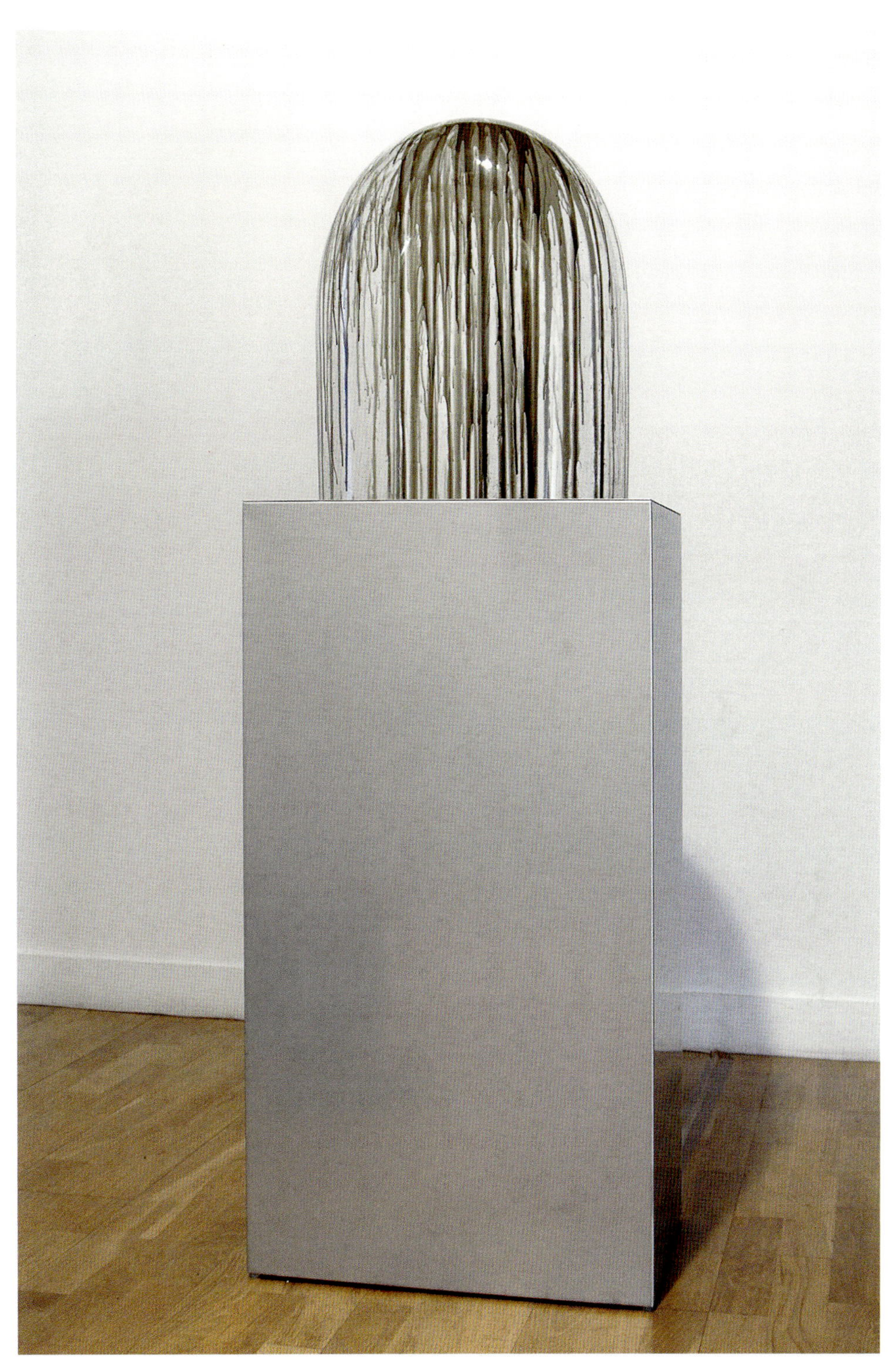

BP, *Untitled*, 1994. Steel, Altuglass, biker suit, electric pump, used motor oil, 235 x 85 x 85 cm. Inv. GR5-L25
BP, *Untitled*, 2002. Steel, glass, electric pump, used motor oil, 138 x 49 x 34 cm. Inv. GR5-L23

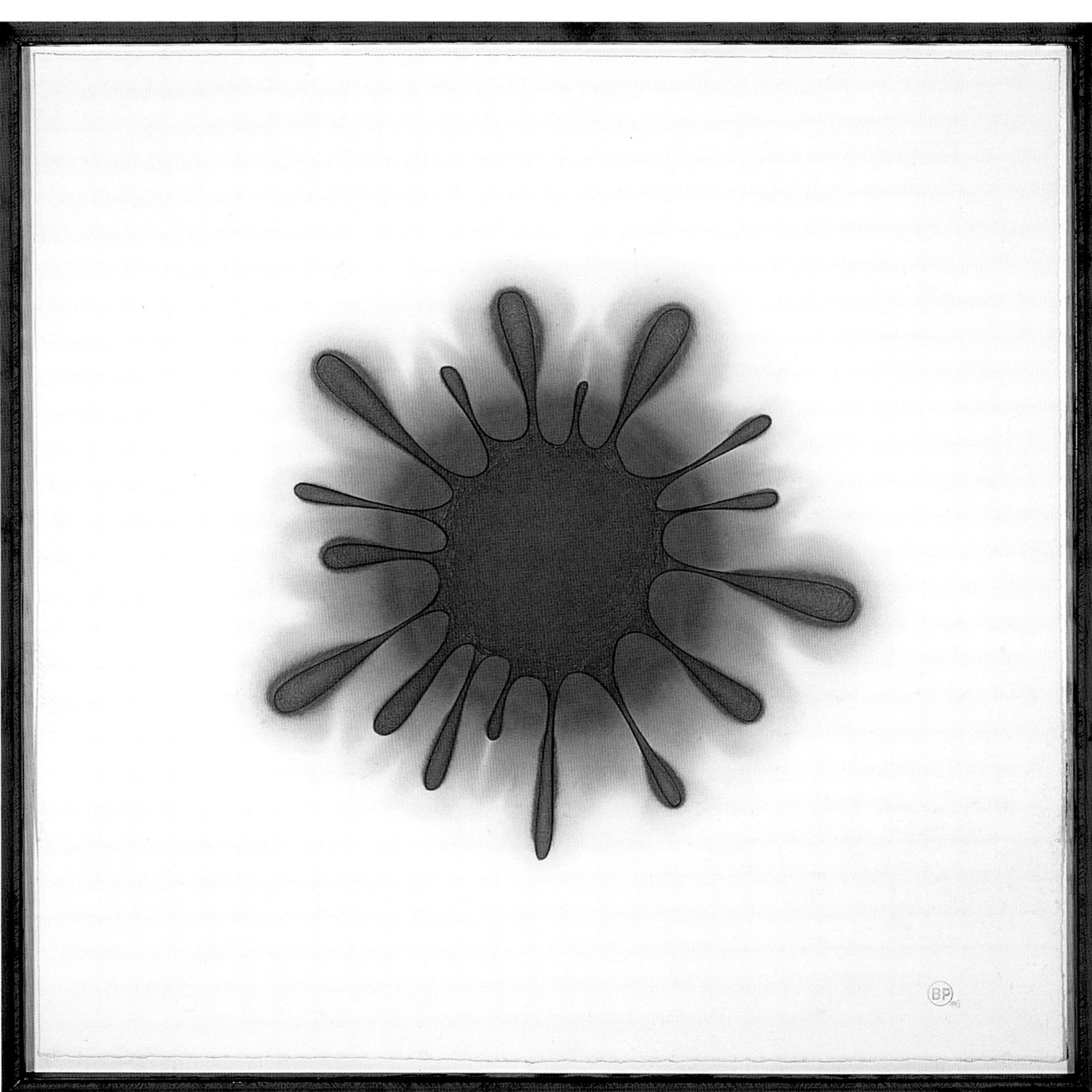

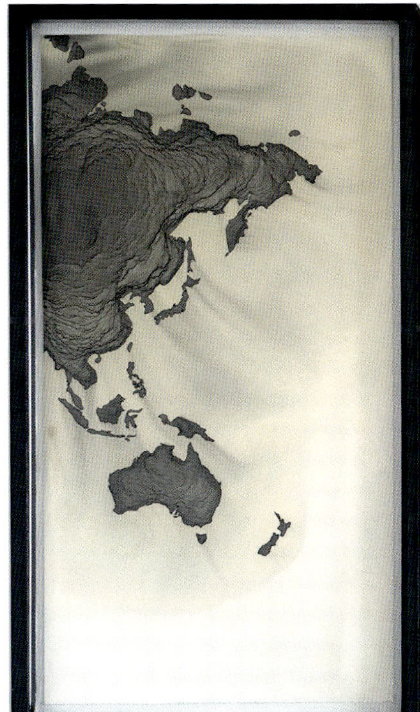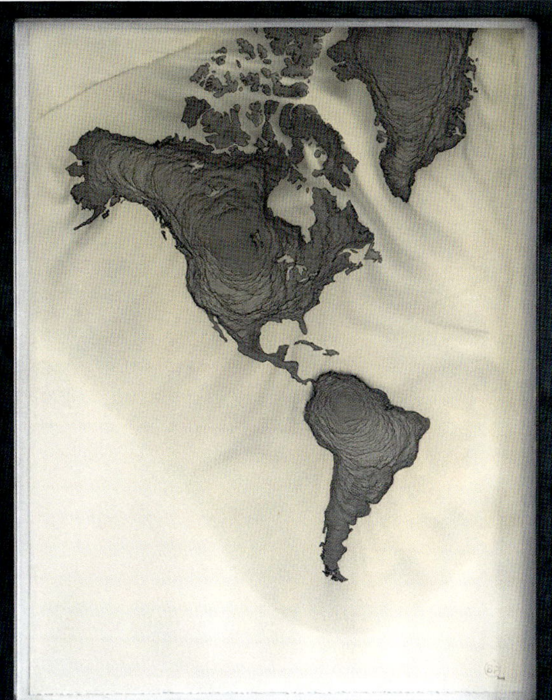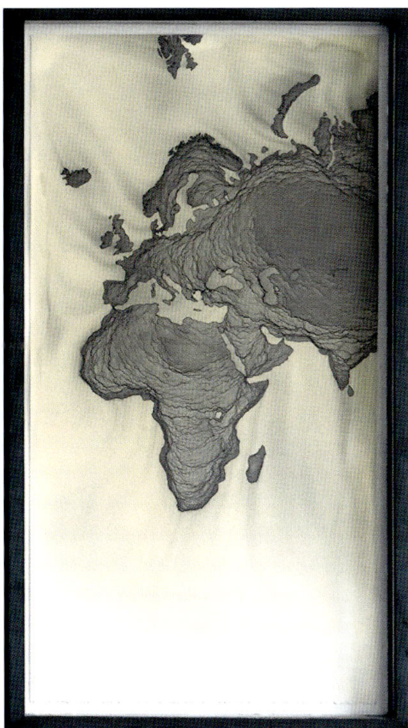

BP, *Splash*, 1998. Graphite, used motor oil on Arches paper, 89 × 89 cm. Inv. GR5-L08
BP, *Map*, 2008. Digital print and used motor oil on Arches paper, steel frame, 167 × 86 × 3 cm. Inv. D432

Following pages
Renaud Layrac, *Pétrographie (archive 1)*, 2022. Digital printing under plexiglass, extruded polystyrene (XPS), 140 × 110 × 8 cm. Inv. GR5-L17
Renaud Layrac, *Pétrographie (archive 2)*, 2022. Digital printing under plexiglass, extruded polystyrene (XPS), 140 × 110 × 8 cm. Inv. GR5-L17

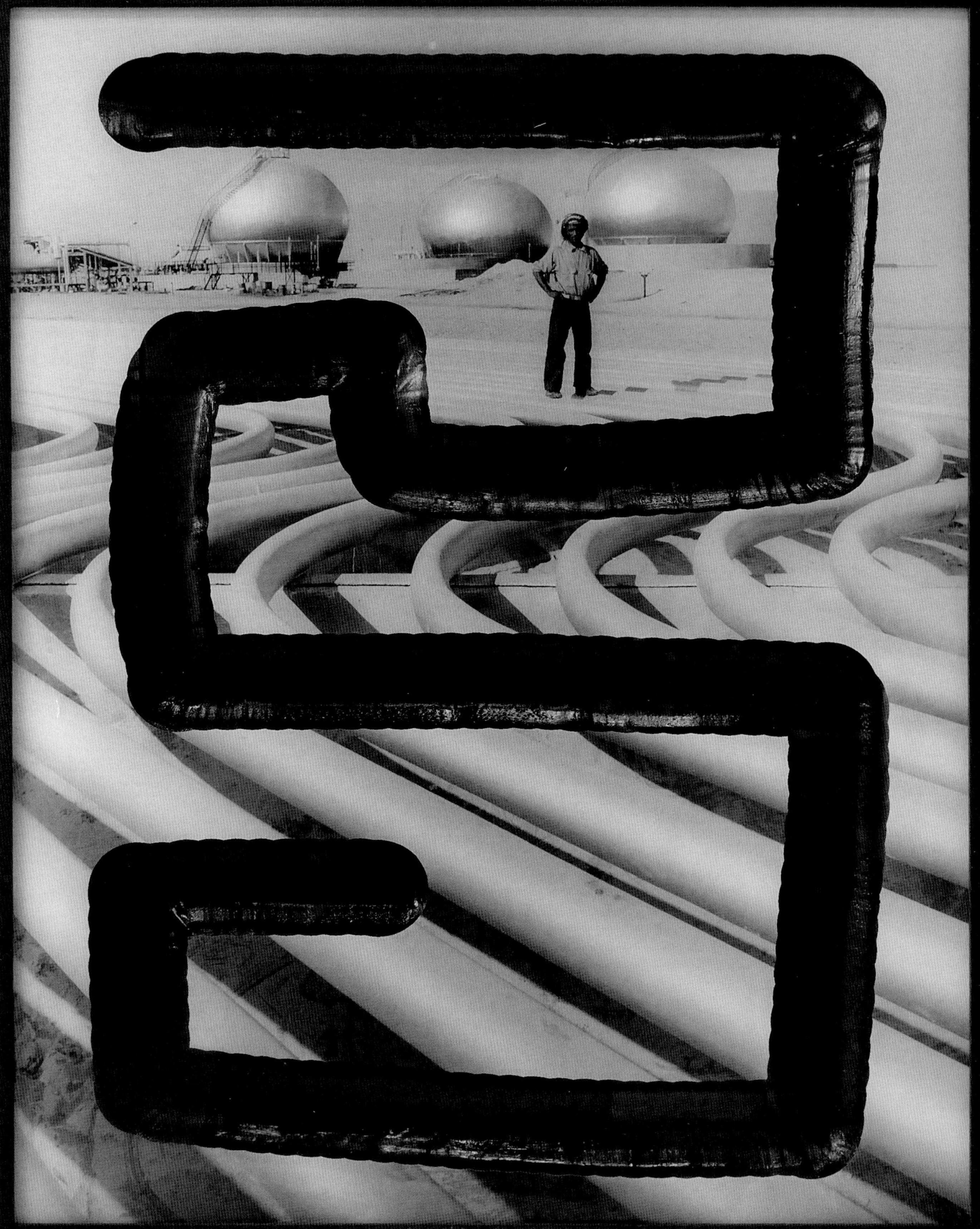

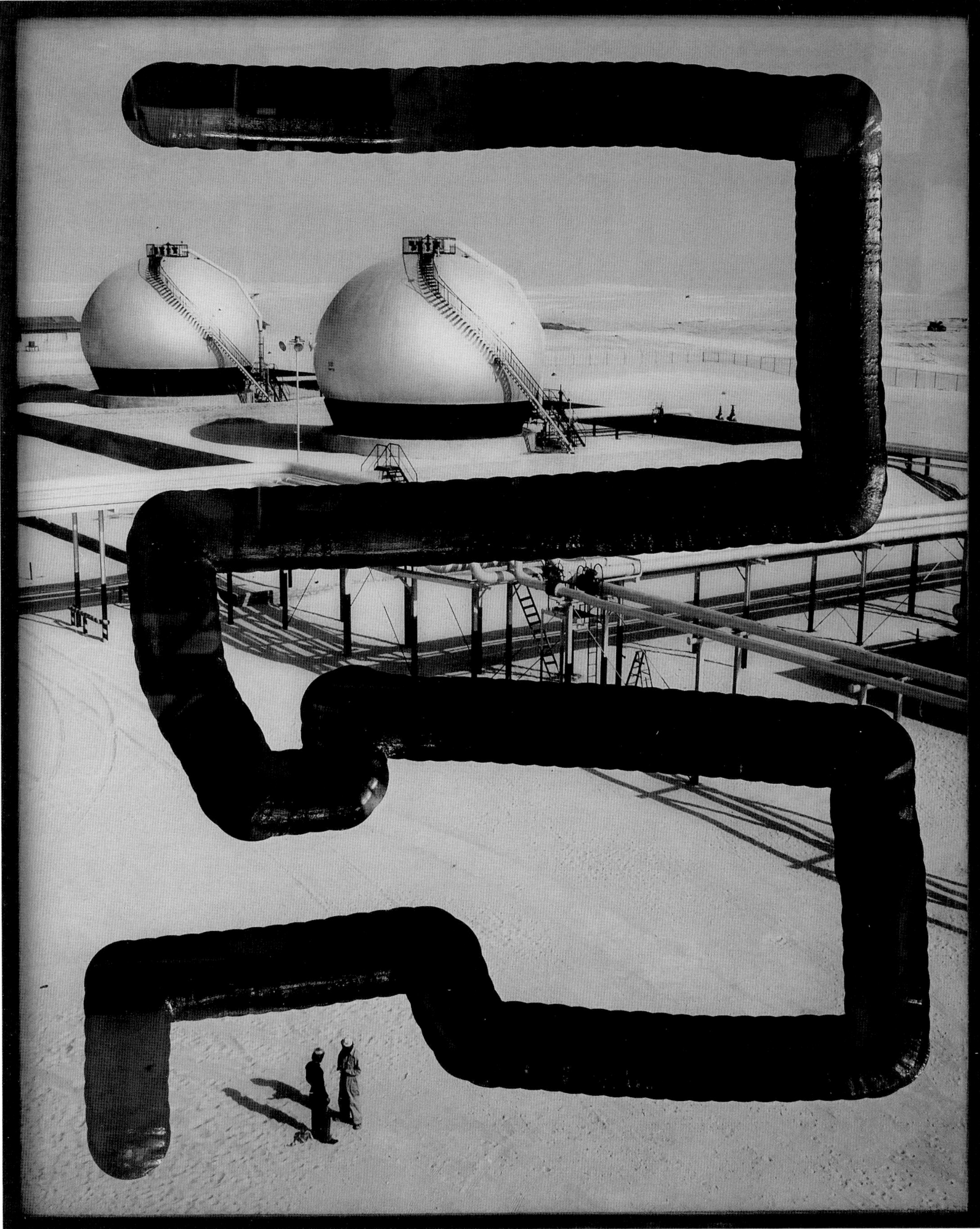

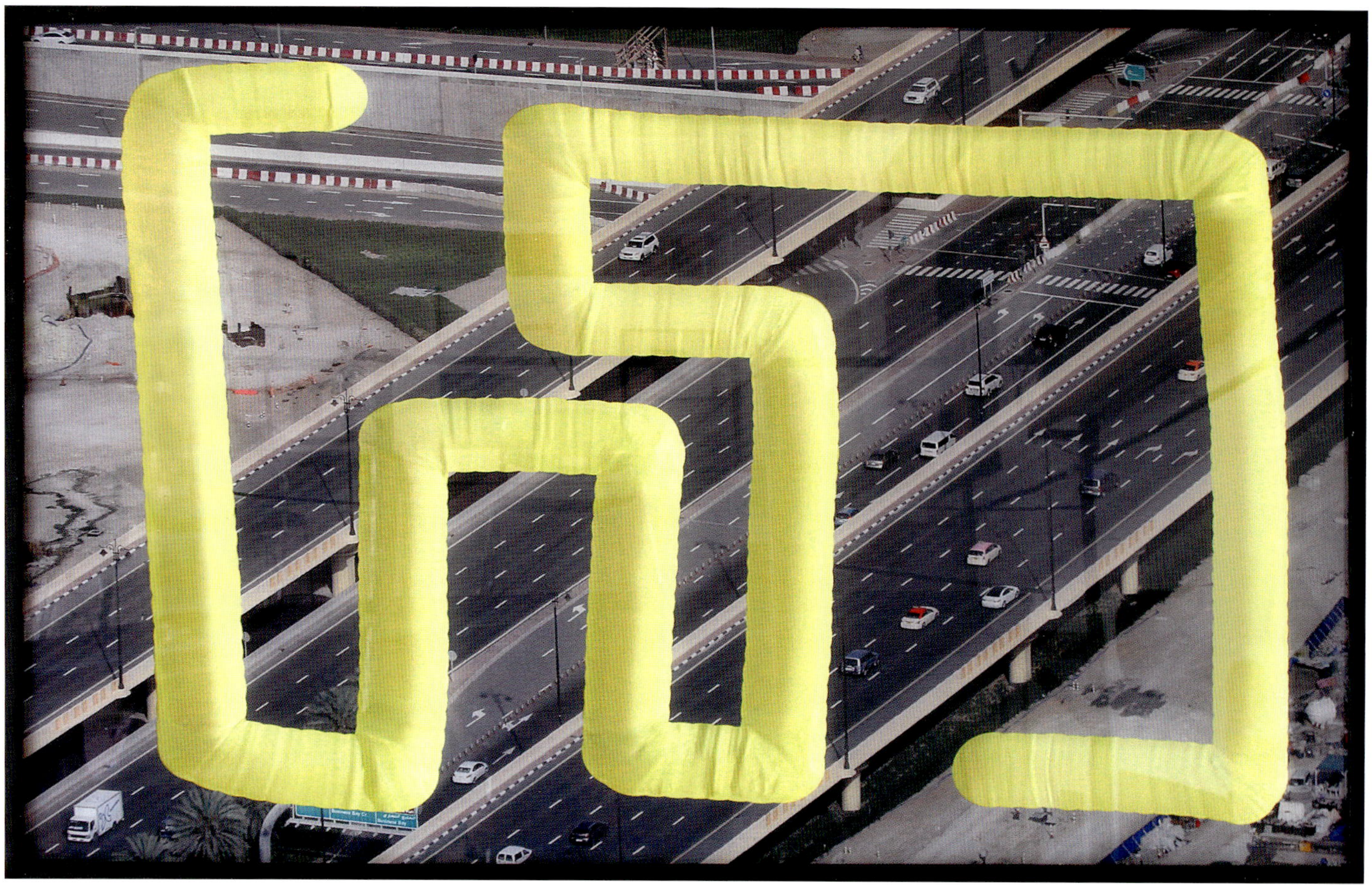

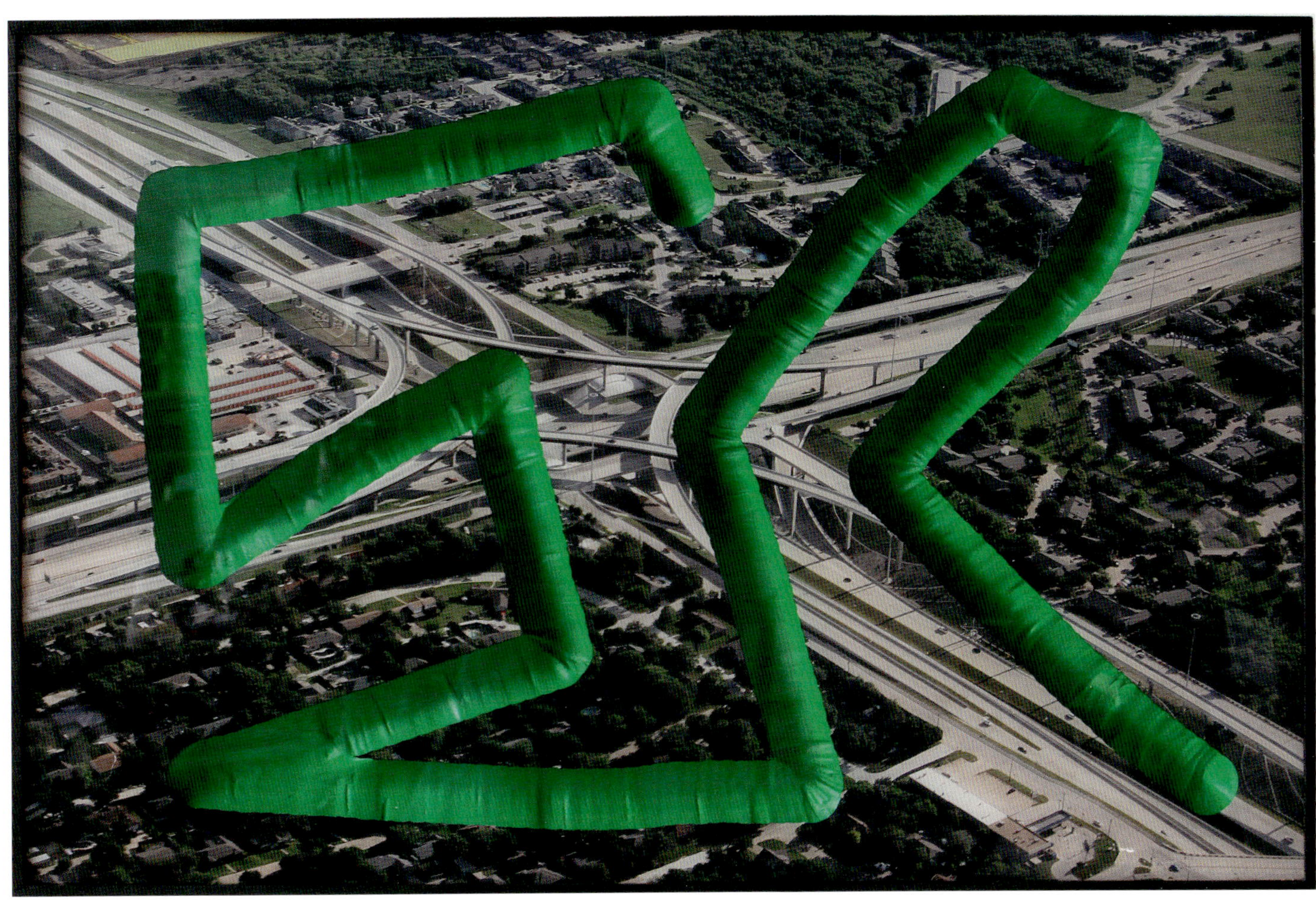

Renaud Layrac. *Untitled*, 2021. Digital print under plexiglass, extruded polystyrene (XPS), 92 × 137 cm. Inv. 3_26_00123
Renaud Layrac. *Untitled*, 2020. Digital print under plexiglass, extruded polystyrene (XPS), 92 × 137 cm. Inv. 3_26_00122

Following pages
Renaud Layrac. *Pétrographie (raffinerie 1)*, 2022. Digital print mounted under plexiglass, extruded polystyrene (XPS), 120 × 179 × 8 cm. Inv. GR5-L16

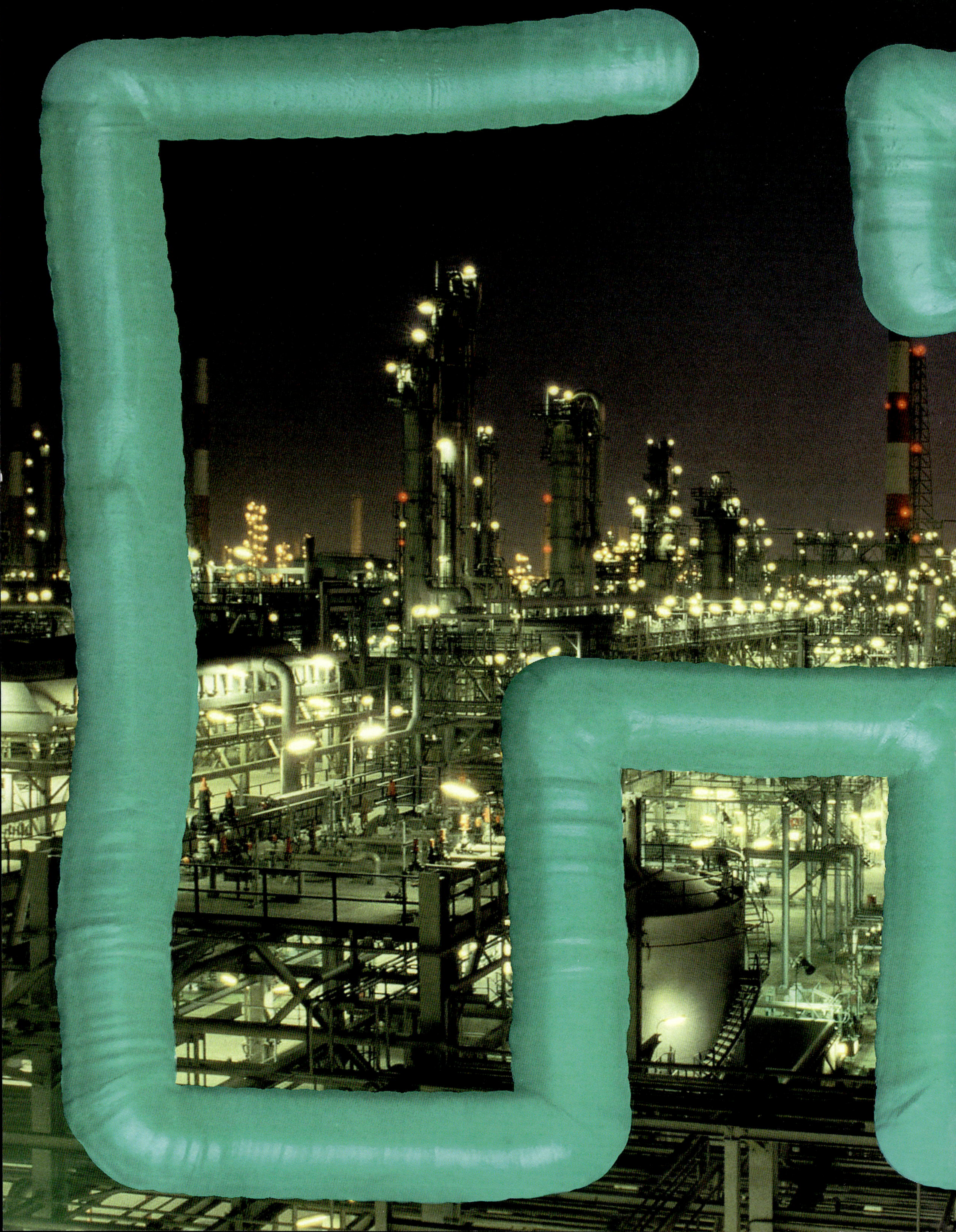

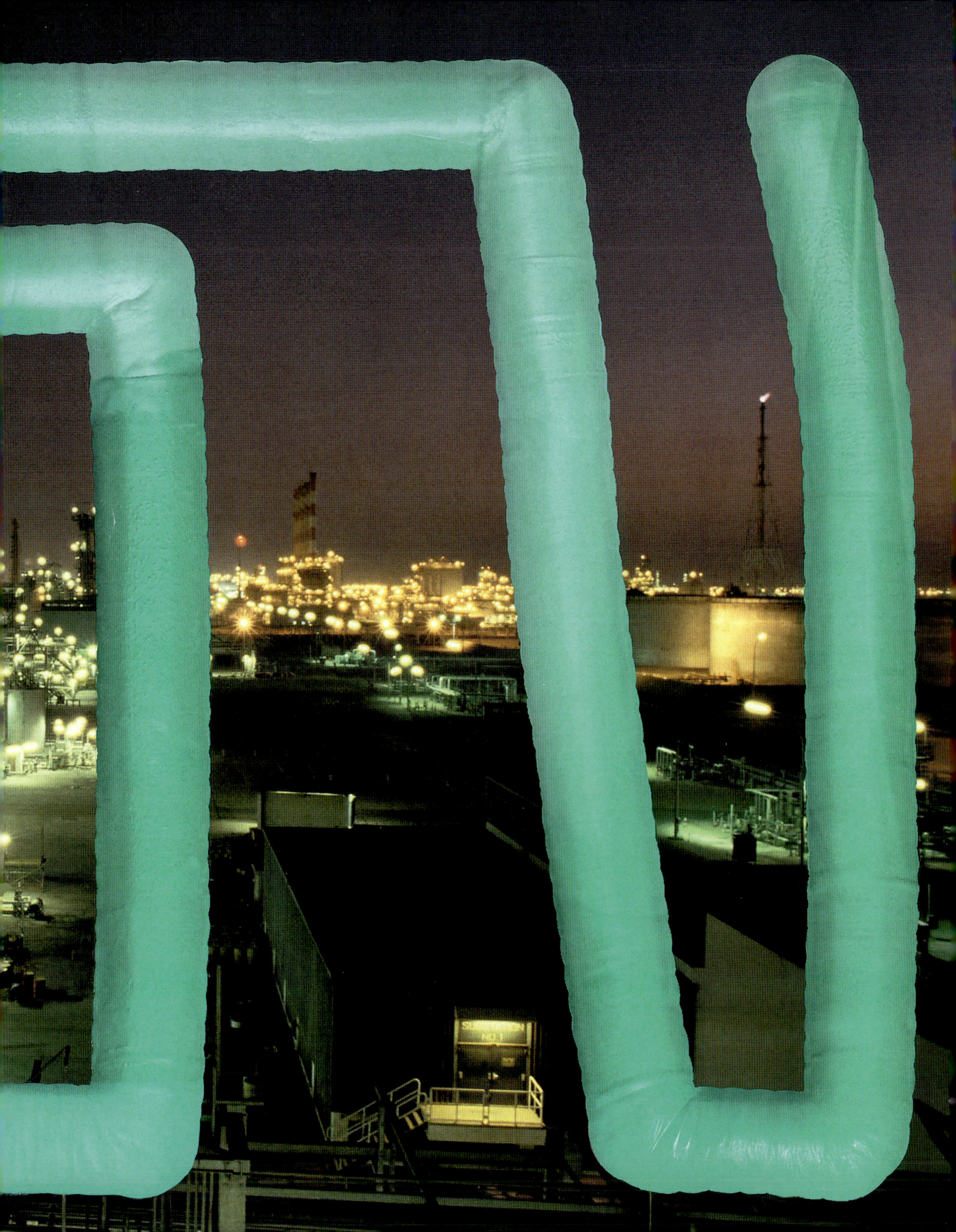

BIOGRAPHIES

Arnauld Pierre is Professor of Art History at Sorbonne University, in Paris. His field of research encompasses the sources and the imaginary of modernity considered in the wider field of scientific and visual culture. An art critic, he has published a number of texts on the revival of modern imaginaries in art today, collected in *Futur antérieur. Art contemporain et rétrocipation* (M19, 2012). As an exhibition curator, he has notably organised the exhibitions *L'Œil moteur. Art optique et cinétique, 1950-1975* (Musée d'art moderne et contemporain de Strasbourg, 2005), *Cosmos. En busca de los orígenes* (TEA, Santa Cruz de Tenerife, 2008), *Nicolas Schöffer* (Musée d'art moderne de Villeneuve-d'Ascq, 2018) and *Victor Vasarely. Le partage des formes* (Centre Pompidou, Paris, 2019, with Michel Gauthier). His latest book, *Magic Moirés. Gerald Oster et l'art des moirages*, was published in 2022 by Macula.

The **BP Collective** was founded in 1984 at the Villa Arson in Nice when Richard Bellon, Renaud Layrac, and Frédéric Pohl met. Eager to break away from traditional forms of individual expression, the three artists decided to collaborate under a common identity, adopting the acronym of the renowned British Petroleum company. Their work draws heavily on industrial and automotive culture, utilizing materials such as waste oil to create critical, sensual installations.

As early as 1986, BP introduced movement into its installations with works in which oil dripped continuously. The group developed a powerful visual language around barrels, crash-test dummies, overalls, and safety equipment, exploring themes related to the body and the machine.

After Bellon's departure in 1991, Layrac and Pohl continued their explorations by combining installations, photography, and collaborations with artists from popular culture.

Until the end of the 2000s, BP exhibited throughout Europe and the United States, pursuing a critical, aesthetic, and committed approach that was always rooted in reflection on the industrial environment and contemporary society.

Renaud Layrac, born in 1962 in Monaco, began his artistic career in 1984 while still a student at Villa Arson in Nice. Nourished by urban culture, the group recycles products from the oil and automobile industries into devices that reinterpret the stereotypes of contemporary art and celebrate the end of avant-garde and modernist utopias.

Since disbanding the collective in 2008, Renaud Layrac has pursued a line of thought in which art, authorship, logos, and signatures confront the worlds of business and communication. His works, whether sculptures or installations, often employ the logic of appropriation and misappropriation. His images question our representation of the world in the age of digital flux: how do we represent, imagine, and understand it?

Involved in higher education, he has participated in research programs with Paris Sorbonne University and also teaches art and scenography at the Fine Arts School in Monaco.

The publication accompanies the exhibition
When Energy Becomes Form, presented at the Black Gold Museum
from 3 December 2025 to 28 February 2026.

Produced by the Museums Commission,
Ministry of Culture, Saudi Arabia and Skira editore.

Head of Business Development
Edoardo Ghizzoni

Managing Editor and Head of Production
Manuela Calandra

Editorial Coordination
Emma Cavazzini, Claudia Podio

Design
Anna Cattaneo

Copyediting
Silvana Bebawy, Sebastiano Siviero

Layout
Sara Marcon

Translations
Adam Victor for Scriptum, Rome

Photo Credits
© All images courtesy of Renaud Layrac, unless mentioned otherwise

Published by Museums Commission,
Ministry of Culture, Saudi Arabia
King Faisal Road, Al Bujairi, Ad Diriyah 13711
Kingdom of Saudi Arabia

Skira editore srl
via Agnello, 18
20121 Milano
Italy
skira-arte.com

ISBN: 978-603-8481-30-1 (Museums Commission)
ISBN: 978-88-572-5044-1 (Skira editore)

This book has been printed by RGM Printing on FSC®-certified paper

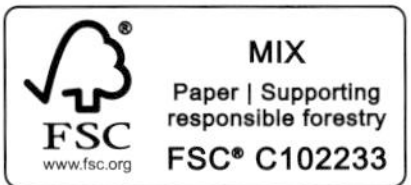

Distributed in USA, Canada, Central & South America
by ARTBOOK | D.A.P., 75 Broad Street Suite 630, New York,
NY 10004, USA.
Distributed elsewhere in the world by Thames and Hudson Ltd,
181A High Holborn, London WC1V 7QX, United Kingdom